# THE ANAPAUSIS PARTNERSHIP

**Common-sense Lessons and Faith-based Principles that Result in a Model of Philanthropy, Mentoring, and Coaching**

## Subesh and Debra Ramjattan

GREEN WINE FAMILY BOOKS
A Division of
GlobalEdAdvancePRESS

**THE ANAPAUSIS PARTNERSHIP**
Common-sense Lessons and Faith-based Principles that Result in a Model of
Philanthropy, Mentoring, and Coaching

Copyright © 2011 by Subesh Ramjattan
Library of Congress Control Number: 2010931994

Ramjattan, Subesh 1951—
The Anapausis Partnership
ISBN 978-1-935434-49-8

Subject Codes and Description: 1: FAM 503040: Family Relations: Marriage
2: BUS 030000—Business and Economics –Business Life-Inspirational;
3:SOC033000: Social Science: Philanthrophy and Charity.

Printed in the USA.

Cover Design by Barton Green

Published by
***GreenWine Family Books***
a division of
GlobalEdAdvance PRESS

# DEDICATION

THIS BOOK IS DEDICATED WITH AFFECTION
TO OUR PARENTS
WHO TAUGHT US COMMON-SENSE LESSONS
AND GUIDED OUR FOOTSTEPS
ON LIFE'S JOURNEY

## ROSIE AND DIPNARINE RAMJATTAN
## ELIVINA AND KENRICK FROST

AND TO THOSE
WHO HAVE JOURNEYED WITH US
IN SUPPORT OF THE VISION OF
BRIDGE OF HOPE AND
THE ANAPAUSIS COMMUNITY.

FUNDS GENERATED FROM THE SALE OF THIS BOOK
WILL GO TO SUPPORT OLIVE'S HOUSE,
A HOUSING COMPLEX FOR SENIORS SERVING AS
SURROGATE GRANDPARENTS FOR THE CHILDREN AT
BRIDGE OF HOPE.

*Can someone truly love God*
*without a love in their heart for others?*

This is the tale of two individuals
who not only recognized the genuine needs
around them, but, in their quest to build a
Bridge of Hope for their world, they fulfilled
what was lacking in each other.

Subesh and Debra Ramjattan taking a campus walk at Anapausis

The Anapausis Partnership is a love story of teamwork
and charity, sacrifice and service, faith and faithfulness.
It is a "How To" treatise both in building a relationship
and advancing an agenda that benefits children,
couples, ministries, NGO'S, non-profit organizations,
and family life... worldwide.

# CONTENTS

**Subesh Ramjattan receiving a Doctor of Humane Letters (DHL)**

THE LOVE GATE

# Author's Preface

**"anapausis"**

When we first heard the word "anapausis" and understood it to mean "refreshing," it caught our attention and was adopted as a construct for our vision of bringing **refreshment** and **happiness** to others. We have come to understand the concept is an informal English transliteration of the Greek construct **"anapsúxeoos"** and **"anapsuxis"** with limited use in the New Testament in two references. In Acts 3:19 normally translated as "refreshing" and another verb form used in 2 Timothy 1:16 translated "refreshed." As with many Greek concepts the word has several meanings depending on the context. In the latter case it seems that Onesiphorus had on more than one occasion "refreshed" his friend Paul. Used in this form it could mean "to cool off, to relieve, to refresh, and to cause to be happy or to make the heart happy. It is also translated as "recovery, revival, renewal, and breathing space." The concept was translated "renewal" in the Devotional New Testament: "Repent and turn back to God, that your sins may be completely cancelled, so that God may grant you a time of **renewal** in the presence of the Lord." (DNT) transliteration: Acts 3:19.

The construct could mean "a state of encouragement after a period of having been troubled or upset; refreshing, recovery of happiness, encouragement; so that times of encouragement will come from the presence of the Lord." The concept tends to suggest "relief, breathing space, renewal, relief from distressful, burdensome circumstances, or so times of relief may come from the Lord or may cause you to have relief from trouble or cause you no longer to be troubled." When one views the broad understanding of the construct, **"Anapausis"** becomes an appropriate word to describe the vision Debbie and I have for our home, homeland and beyond. **We desire to bring relief to the needy and encouragement to the weary.** This is demonstrated in various projects to benefit needy children and a conference compound to house several nonprofit entities that become the venue for different faith-based meetings.

We use "anapausis" for the name of our home, to describe the vision, to provide identity for the conference compound, and to name the Greek-letter Society structured to preserve and perpetuate our legacy. Membership in the Society is by invitation based on an understanding of the vision, the mission, and the antecedent cause that initiated the burden for Trinidad and Tobago.

# THE ANAPAUSIS SOCIETY

## TAU ALPHA SIGMA
# ΤΑΣ

THE ANAPAUSIS SOCIETY (TAU ALPHA SIGMA--- ΤΑΣ), is a Greek-letter Society to foster the vision and fulfill the mission we have initiated. Membership in the Society is by invitation and classified by levels of participation as **ALPHA (A), BETA (B)** or **OMEGA (Ω).** Both couples and individuals will be enrolled and tutored in the mission and antecedent cause that initiated the vision, guided the projects and developed the ideals the Society is designed to perpetuate. Members will be exposed to the common-sense lessons, practical business practices, and the faith-based principles which have guided our lives and enterprises with the hope that these will become factors in their lives and work. These individuals will be asked to sign a Society Register, make a Pledge of Fidelity and a faith-promise to participate in the ongoing work of the Society as family and business permit.

**--Subesh and Debra Ramjattan**

THE LOVE GATE

# Foreword

Subesh Ramjattan takes us on a journey of inspiration and hope that the words and deeds of one can change the lives of many. From his humble beginnings in the village of Plum Mitan, to leading a business empire, to his ordination as a minister of God, Subesh has traveled a road with many challenges and his book is a touchingly honest compilation of the lessons that he wishes to leave as part of his legacy.

Subesh's transition to a life of service to others has encouraged many of those whose lives he has touched to search for what is better within us. He has over the past 10 – 15 years walked in the footsteps of the Lord Jesus Christ as a servant leader, yet his message has never been one of admonishment or sanction, but rather the compassion and empathy of a brother and father. I am sure Subesh's book will cause the reader to reflect on how each of us can channel our talents and blessings in the service of mankind while understanding that this is not an easy route but one requiring understanding, love and faith. Subesh shows us that despite the many challenges and disappointments that we may face in the service of others, it is our faith and belief in a higher purpose that can sustain us.

Subesh's message in this book appeals across religious persuasions, class and the other divides that we have used to separate and differentiate ourselves from our brothers and sisters. This book offers a view of how we can transform our personal struggles and tribulations into a force for positive change in our families, in our work places, in our communities and in our nation. We are reminded that there will be disappointments and sorrow on the way but that love for one another does prevail. Subesh accomplishes his quest to impart a living legacy to those that will follow by providing practical and real examples of how investing in lives generates a powerful force for change. He shares with us insights into the lives and hearts of those who have journeyed with him, infusing us with the hope that as children of God, whatever our circumstances, we can with will, constancy and belief triumph over the frailty and imperfections that make us innately human.

This work is a tribute to Subesh's courage and tenacity and his success in fusing his common-sense approach and business acumen acquired in his search for success in the secular world with the teachings and belief in a higher order which guides his later years. This book represents Subesh's desire to reach beyond the communities and forums in which he operates to connect his ideas and approaches with a wider audience, in the hope that others can come to believe and trust in their power to effect positive change. As a non Christian and one who is spiritually ambiguous, I have had the honor and privilege of calling this great and humble man my friend and mentor. There is no time in the 15 years of our friendship that Subesh has not taken the time to listen and offer support or counsel for my own challenges however small they may seem. He inspires me to seek for the strength and resolve to become a better person and to direct the talents that I may have to the service of others.

This book allows readers to gain that inspiration and to share in the solutions that can lead to a happier and more fulfilling life. Over the years, Subesh has spoken and connected with persons of every walk of life, from statesman to beggar, and as a servant leader his message, actions and infinite empathy are a source of strength, peace and motivation to all. As we have been blessed to be part of this great man's life, readers across this country, in the region and across the globe have an opportunity to know and love this humble, gentle and inspirational man, and to **understand that through a life of service we can advance the cause of goodness and justice.**

Follow Subesh in his personal and compelling account of the force of positive transformation as he seeks to effect change and bring hope to this nation, one person, one family and one community at a time. May God bless you, brother Subesh, and may this book inspire others to find an opportunity to apply the compelling lessons and legacy you have shared.

**--Vashtie Dookiesingh,**
**Inter-American Development Bank**

THE LOVE GATE

# PUBLISHER'S INTRODUCTION

## *PARTNERSHIP WITH GOD AND OTHERS*

### A Remarkable Man

Subesh Ramjattan is a remarkable man who is hungry for knowledge and reaches for every kernel of truth he can find from any source. His life's journey began in a poor village learning common-sense lessons from his family and the village environment. He proceeded to learn more in school and as a young man worked hard to gather both the knowledge and the resources needed to start his own business. He listens attentively to anyone who speaks and he reads everything in sight. Subesh remembers almost everything good he hears, sees, or learns from any source. He is much the same as a working honey bee constantly busy going from flower to flower gathering sweet nectar and returning to his own sheltered nest to spend the collected nectar into his own honey. When these various components are formed into a new whole, they become his personally discovered treasure.

### A Brilliant Student

Subesh is similar to a brilliant student who quietly discovers the interrelationships of facts and believes he is the only one in the world who has uncovered this hidden truth. He learns various things and mixes them together in his subconscious and creates a jewel of great price. He attributes great value to what he has learned and combines all the facts to produce principles for life and work. When his brain has synthesized these facts into common-sense lessons and/or faith-based principles, they become his intellectual treasure which he is driven to share with others.

## A Common Man for the Common Good

The same eagerness with which these kernels of truth were gathered and processed is the same passion used to produce lessons for life, productive businesses, and projects to serve the less fortunate. It was this insight that birthed the "anapausis" vision, this enthusiasm that built the Bridge of Hope custodial care facility and the attendant community services, and brought into being the Anapausis Compound, a faith-based community that provides facilities and venues to serve the common good of the people.

## "Auntie Debbie"

His partner in love, life, and mission is Debra, better known as "Auntie Debbie" by the disadvantaged children she unselfishly serves with her husband. She is a beautiful and talented helpmate who shares a commitment to faith-based principles and a special ministry to those in need. Debbie's zeal for the children produces a desire to meet them at their point of need regardless of the cost in time and treasure. She also learned common-sense lessons in a small village in Trinidad and gleaned certain values from her early years of working with the general public. These concepts combined with her faith make her compatible with the faith-based principles she and Subesh use to guide their lives, business, and service to others.

## A Story of Teamwork and Charity

This partnership is a love story of teamwork and charity, sacrifice and service, faith and faithfulness. This book is a tale of two individuals who not only recognized the needs around them, but, in their quest to create business ventures to support the common good, they **built a bridge of hope for the needy and a place called "anapausis" to refresh believers**. This partnership fulfilled what was lacking in each other, gathered other partners who shared the same vision, and produced great benefit for Trinidad and Tobago and the regions beyond.   This story validates the saying that "two are better than one and that a three-fold cord is not easily broken!"

**One God plus Two People**
This book is about two people and how they teamed up together with God and others to fulfill a mission to assist their homeland of Trinidad and Tobago. It is a narrative of love and work, faith and worship, sacrament and service, stewardship and charity, teamwork and faithfulness. The pages are filled with common-sense lessons that are later sanctified into faith-based principles and used to advance many projects for the benefit of their homeland.  The big question: **Can anyone really love God without a love in their heart for others?**

**Unselfish Love is the Foundation**
Love then is the foundation of this story.  God started with one man, but decided he needed a helpmate.  This narrative starts in two rural villages of Trinidad, West Indies, and becomes the love story of a man and a women working together and teaming with God and others to advance an agenda that benefits children, couples, ministries, non-profit organizations, NGO's, and government entities related to education, childcare, and family life. The account begins in the villages of Plum Mitan and Williamsville.

**The Construct of Partnership**
The voice at Creation declared, **"It is not good for man to be alone"** and common sense speaks to the dilemma of loneliness and solitude.  **Everyday people understand that**

**when one gets tired doing nothing there is no place to stop and rest; therefore, hard work leads to good rest.** The ancient Talmud added to the record "A man without companions is like the left hand without the right." And a wise man in sacred writings declared, "Two are better than one for they have a good reward for their labor."

> **Two are better than one;**
> **Because they have a good reward for their labour.**
> **For if they fall, the one will lift up his fellow:**
> **but woe to him that is alone when he falleth;**
> **for he hath not another to help him up.**
> **Again, if two lie together, then they have heat:**
> **but how can one be warm alone?**
> **And if one prevail against him, two shall withstand him;**
> **and a threefold cord is not quickly broken.**
> (Eccl 4:9-12 KJV)

## A Business Partnership

A successful businessman with three businesses in Miami, Florida and four in Trinidad and Tobago, Subesh worked 15-hour stress filled days. As a new believer in the Christian faith, he was not pleased with his life. A renewed focus on his children and a 12-week new believer's class assisted Subesh Ramjattan with a prayer for a vision. **"God, show me where your cause needs me most."** was his prayer. **He desired to live a life larger than himself and work together with God in the areas of the greatest need.** He decided that his workaholic temperament could be an advantage to Kingdom building. Money could not purchase happiness, but there was a good reward for hard work especially when the bottom line was used to assist the less fortunate.

## The Need for a Life Partner

At first Subesh thought he would give to support the ministry and charitable work of others, then the realization came that his personal business talents were needed to produce constructive projects to serve the disadvantaged. He yearned for a more fruitful and fulfilling personal life and to do what he could to change the world for the better. Subesh knew he needed a faithful life partner to accomplish his lofty goals. This became part of his daily prayer.

## Married on Christmas Day

In January 1994, Subesh moved back to his homeland of Trinidad and Tobago. There he met Debra Frost, the daughter of a business associate. She was a native Trinidadian who had recently returned from Washington, D.C., where she worked for the Australian Embassy. Debra was beautiful and independent and best of all she was a woman of faith. They began courting and the relationship blossomed. After six months, in the shade of a coconut tree, Subesh asked Debra to be his life partner. They were married on December 25, 1994—celebrating their marriage along with the birth of their Savior. It was a new beginning for Subesh. He relished having a wife as a prayer partner and decided to visit the Holy Land. They were baptized in the Jordan River to place a seal on their new relationship. On the banks of the muddy Jordan River and under the clear Caribbean moon, the vision and mission of this new partnership began to creep out of the shadows into the bright Caribbean sunlight.

## A Gift from God

Subesh and Debra had the normal relationship ups and downs as they adjusted to their new life together. Providentially, they met Steve and Cecilia Mohammed, on staff with Campus Crusade for Christ in Trinidad, and learned several marriage principles from FamilyLife, a marriage and family subsidiary of Campus Crusade. One principle that proved beneficial was **"your spouse is a gift from God and not your enemy."** Both came to realize that their spouse was not just a guest at the wedding but were heaven-sent partners for life and a true gift from God. This knowledge brought the cherished warmth needed to strengthen the marriage relationship for the work God had called them both to do in their homeland.

**"And may the Lord increase you and cause you to abound in love one toward another, and toward all, even as we do toward you: 13. In order that he may strengthen your hearts..."** --1 Thessalonians 12,13a (DNT)

## Common-sense Lessons

The common-sense lessons in this book speak directly to the issues that produced the Anapausis Partnership, the Bridge of Hope network, FamilyLife Projects, Educational Testing Services, OASIS UNIVERSITY, the International Children's Academy for Neurodevelopment (I CAN) and a new school project for the Village of Kernahan, a rural village with about 150 families and an estimated 35 children ages 3-5 without a pre-school. On donated land and with partnership of a major company in Trinidad and Tobago, this village and these pre-school children now have a debt-free school and community centre. As others join this partnership, more will be accomplished.

## Always Searching

Subesh and Debbie are always searching for new ideas and continue to explore ways and means to serve with creative minds and hearts. They are a team but desire to partner with others to better serve their homeland. They express gratitude for the contributions and encouragement from corporate sponsors and friends who assist in supporting the less fortunate. One goal of the Ramjattans is to gather a group of "alpha" individuals into The Anapausis Society and pass on to them all they have learned. They desire to transfer their vision and create a sustainable endeavor for Trinidad and Tobago. They hope to leave a legacy of good stewardship and service to the needy of their homeland. The vision reaches the Caribbean region and extends to those living in poverty around the world.

## The Foundation Stones

From where did this vision come? The foundation stones were laid in childhood in separate villages in Trinidad, cultivated in hard work and youthful struggles, and culminated in an understanding that it was better to nurture a needy child than to put back together the pieces of a broken adult. Your assistance is needed to preserve this vision and continue beneficial projects to assist the needy. Will you become a partner of the "anapausis vision" and help preserve the legacy?　**---Hollis L. Green, ThD, PhD, Publisher**

**The future,
of children and the Nation of**

**Trinidad and Tobago,
is in your hands!**

THE LOVE GATE

# CHAPTER ONE

## *EARLY CHILDHOOD IN TRINIDAD*

### The Village of Plum Mitan

**My life's journey began in the village of Plum Mitan.** I was born to Rosie and Dipnarine Ramjattan in this rural agricultural village on the eastern seaboard of Trinidad and Tobago. My family included seven brothers and two sisters. Life in the village was not a bed of roses. It was filled with poor families with few comforts of home or access to community services. The village had no running water or electricity and used kerosene lamps for light. The farmers were poor but worked hard and grew watermelon, rice, bananas, ground provisions, and indigenous fruits and vegetables. They caught "cascadura" and other fresh water fish for sale and personal use.

### No Running Water
We made "box-carts" and brought water from the only well in the village. The villagers were up by 3:00 am waiting to collect their water supply from the water trucks. This still happens today in 2010. The villagers shared their resources with each other – if one family had corn they shared and got in return peas, bread, cakes, etc... There were no burglaries

and no need for burglar-proof windows when I was growing up in Plum Mitan. At the time of this writing there is still no running water in my village.

## Morning Life in the Village
Village life was hectic each morning, with the sounds of farmers going to the fields and the lagoon to work. My father was up at 4:00 a.m. each day to drive a garbage truck. My father was a man of quick temper and when something did not go just right, especially when he was getting ready to go to work, we saw a different side of this normally kind, helpful and generous person. At times the old garbage truck number TD-3613 would not start and my brothers, neighbors and I would push the truck down the hill until it started. My mother and grandmother were also up at the crack of dawn to prepare lunches packed in brown bags for school.

## 16 Ounces was 16 Ounces
My mother was also a charitable person. I recall her giving raw flour and baking powder to villagers to make "roti" and she would bring them to the house for some salted butter to eat with their "roti." A typical breakfast meal in the countryside was Sada roti and butter with tea. My mother operated a shop and bar in the front of our house which was also the local post office. Honesty and integrity were my parents' work ethics "16 ounces was 16 ounces."

## My Mother was the Listener
Low self esteem and shyness made introductions to others difficult, especially to the opposite sex. It was hard for me to share my challenges with my father since he always seemed to be working. My mother was the listener in the midst of her busyness. She was a good homemaker and also had time to do her post office job for which she got TT$100.00 per month and also attend to the grocery and bar, not forgetting the many families in the community she fed and sewed their

clothes. If you ask mother how she did this, the response would be **"only by God's Grace."**

## Earning Spending Money

My two older brothers, younger sisters and I grew watermelons in the Nariva Swamp. Holiday time for us was spent in the cocoa and coffee fields. We were also rice growers, so we milled rice in our rice mill and milled rice for others for about a penny a pound. In order to earn extra money my eldest brother would borrow my father's vehicle to transport the local fishermen to the market. He got up at 1:00 a.m. on Sundays to accomplish this task. These efforts gave us spending money for school and we learned common-sense lessons from the ventures.

## Sharing and Giving

The common-sense lesson of sharing and giving from the heart was an early lesson learned from my family. My parents were always able to manage with what little they had, and I saw what we had multiplied as they fed many others – we always had just what we needed and no more until the next time. John Wesley, a great religious leader, said:

**"Do all the good you can; by all the means you can,**
**In all the ways you can; in all the places you can,**
**At all the times you can; as long as ever you can."**

My parents certainly lived up to this and in the midst of hardships passed it on to their children.

## Lessons of Working Together

The village families shared what they had and taught the children the valued lessons of working together and helping others. The children worked alongside the adults in the watermelon fields and the rice fields and picked bananas, coffee and cocoa and learned the value of working together and that hard work was a necessary part of village life. There were few prospects, no government subsidies, and the village farmers were left to labor and fend for themselves. Each family got along the best they could with what they had, but there was love and concern for one another. Uppermost in the minds of all were the needs of the children and the family.

## Things Learned from Isolation

My rural village suffered from the evils of isolation and learned early the need for cooperation and teamwork. Villagers realized that the joint labors of two produced more than the efforts of a solitary worker. From this the children learned that companionship and teamwork were both supportive and profitable. These were common-sense lessons learned by the children from daily life in the village and this practical training enabled the children to realize the value of family and friends.

## Early Instructions in Morality and Ethics

I attended Plum Mitan Presbyterian School in the village and received foundational instructions in morality and ethics. These dedicated teachers also planted a few seeds of truth in my young life. They understood early childhood development and that education comes from the Latin **e duc** meaning "to lead out or draw out" and suggested taking children by the hand and leading them into an understanding of the subject at hand. These teachers were committed and assisted my early growth and development. I studied by kerosene lamps and homemade flambeaux lights made from bottles filled with kerosene using pieces of burlap bags as wicks. Learning was exciting and each new understanding brightened my hopes for a better life.

## Early Common-sense Lessons

At the Presbyterian School, I was exposed to organized athletics and acquired an understanding of the rules and regulations of cricket, football, and other team sports. These foundation rules of teamwork, cooperation, and the desire to play fair and win were early common-sense lessons that have stayed with me into adulthood. I was the only student in 1962 who passed the Common Entrance examinations to secure a place at North Eastern College, a 7-year reputable academic program in Sangre Grande. Village transport was a big problem since only one bus left for Sangre Grande at 6:00 a.m. and returned at 4:00 p.m. If you missed the bus either way, it made life difficult. My grandparents lived in the village of Upper Manzanilla and agreed to house me during the week so I could attend school. I went home on weekends to catch up on chores and be with my family.

**A Hard Working Grandfather**
My grandfather was a hardworking man. He planted cocoa, coffee and copra and groomed and trained race horses. He lived one mile from the beach and this allowed me to groom and race the horses on the beach and swim with them. I was able to join others to prepare the cocoa for the market. This was done by spreading the dried cocoa in a proper place and pouring on some water and oil and everyone would tromp with their feet. This was called "dance the cocoa." It was both fun and work and I received 25 cents for this task. The lesson that work could be fun and that working hard for what was needed, was vital to my future. I learned at an early age **"from the sweat of thy brow thou shall eat bread."** Hard work was necessary for what was needed and I also learned to appreciate and take better care of the things purchased with earned money.

**Learning to Surmount Difficulties**
Small rural communities develop a friendliness that sur-mounts difficulties and breeds hospitability and warmth. This becomes a therapy and medication for many ills produced by poverty. Such interaction of community spirit creates a good reward for a labor intensive culture. At times kindness

becomes a reward in itself, and the children of the village form lasting friendships. There is no end to the benefits of true friendship. In fact, friends are better than money in the bank. One can have access to the interest without diminishing the value and resource of the principal friendship. Such relationships with friends and family provide assistance in emergencies, supply daily mutual support for families, and gives additional strength for both the tasks at hand and the hard journey ahead. I will always be grateful to my family and the people in the village of Plum Mitan. My memory of village life was a tug at my heart that pulled me back to Trinidad and Tobago.

## The Village of Williamsville

**My life began as Debra Frost.** I was born to ambitious parents,
 Elivina and Kenrick Frost, in the rural Village of Williamsville, located in South Trinidad. My father was just an apprentice learning a trade and eventually became an auto mechanic. My mother was about to enter teacher's training college when she met and fell in love with my father. Mother was a self-made business woman who still owns and operates a profitable business and was the first female customs broker in Trinidad and Tobago and the Caribbean region.

### Growing-up Lessons

My parents worked hard at their jobs and were fruitful. Like every other family, we had hard times. From this experience I learned the value of sharing, proper hygiene, eating the same thing that others ate, and sharing hand-me-down clothes. My parents kept a clean domestic environment, so I had to keep my room clean and make my bed on rising. I am an early riser so I would watch the sugar cane farmers with their food bags and cutlasses on their way to work at sunrise and then returning late in the evening. I learned to appreciate those who worked the soil. This together with working in our family garden gave me an appreciation for animal and plant life and every living and growing thing.

## Good Housekeeping Guidelines
I learned good housekeeping skills during the growing years from my parents. We learned from our parents in the garden, planting, nurturing, reaping and admiring beauty and watching things grow with patience. These experiences added value to my life and were good lessons that prepared me to see both the necessity of hard work and that the effort produced good rewards for the labor.

## Play and Work
Community life in Williamsville taught me valuable life lessons which gave me a good foundation and prepared me for life. Families shared crops, food, favors, and when one household was sick each neighbor was a helping and healing hand. Neither race nor religion divided the people. The village gave me a good foundation and preparation for life. Children played with each other without prejudice. Playtime was a great gift and all the children learned from play and work.

## A Singing Grandmother
My interest in music was inspired by my grandmother. I developed an early interest in music because grandmother was an excellent singer and would wake up the whole village with her singing at about 4:00 a.m. in the morning while she cooked and did yard work. However, my music development was hindered by family needs and limited access to further education. There were no funds for music lessons, but finally mother purchased an old guitar for me.

## A One Dollar One String Guitar
It is hard to estimate the worth and long-term value of a one string guitar that cost only one dollar. Since a gift is valued

regulations of teamwork, cooperation, and the desire to play fair and win.

❖ There is no end to the benefit of true friendship.

❖ Learning the value of sharing, proper hygiene, eating the same thing that others ate, and wearing hand me downs for clothes are good lessons for life.

❖ Rising early each morning to see men going to work prepared to provide an honest day's labor is a positive lesson for future employment.

❖ Personally working in the family garden provides an appreciation for living and growing things.

❖ Learning good housekeeping during the growing years is a lesson with great benefits.

❖ Neither race nor religion should divide the people.

❖ A good foundation for life is to value family and neighbors.

❖ Sharing what one has with others is part of an honest life.

❖ Playtime is a great gift to the children when they learn to play without prejudice.

❖ Sacrificial gifts of parents teach valuable lessons to the children.

❖ A gift is valued by what it costs the giver.

❖ Learning that life has a single focus provides a life without distractions.

❖ Patience is a virtue children must learn early.

❖ Learning the value of music, love, and laughter is necessary for a productive life.

❖ Learning the value of work and the worth of money is required for mature living.

❖ Learning to earn, save, and spend money provides a good foundation for life.

❖ Energy spent in a task increases the value of the coin the labor produces.

❖ There is no free lunch. One must earn his bread by honest labor.

❖ Practical lessons learned from grandparents are things children may never acquire in school.

❖ Many of the hard lessons learned as children become the valued basis for moral and ethical living as an adult

❖ Lessons from the previous generation are always seasoned with experience and mixed with genuine affection.

❖ Grandparents have a special ability to imprint their character and morality on their grandchildren.

THE LOVE GATE

# CHAPTER TWO

## *YEARS OF YOUTHFUL STRUGGLE*

### Youthful Struggle

**As a young man my journey** from Plum Mitan to developing  studies and work experience was not an easy one. Having won placement in Northeastern College, there were two main difficulties: first, after chores there was little space or time in a small house with a large family for study by kerosene lamps; second, there was limited transportation from the village to the one 6 a.m. bus. Studying by lamp light and walking to the bus in the early darkness, I learned courage and perseverance to achieve five academic O-Levels, including one in the Principles of Business and Accounting. This became the foundation and motivation for me as a young man to venture out into the larger world and dream of personally owning and operating my own business.

### Employment and Destiny

At age 18, with my parents blessings, a brown bag containing some clothes and food, and the generous gift of my father's last five dollars, I ventured out of the secure little village to the wiles of Port of Spain, the capital city, to seek employment and my destiny. With a tearful family parting and five dollars in my pocket, my father asked me to make a simple promise: "Never steal from anyone." Contained in the limited family resources represented by the five dollars and the moral promise never to take advantage of others by stealing was the essence of morality for my life and my practice of business.  I did not have many skills but was willing and eager and common sense prevailed.  With limited confidence I ventured into the unknown world in search of my purpose in life with the moral integrity to earn the resources to build my own business.  The common-sense lesson that "Honesty is the best policy in life and business" has been a main stay for the faith-based principles used in business operations through the years.

**Salvation Army Hostel**
In Port of Spain, I rented a bed/cot in the Salvation Army Hostel and this was my space for a while.  In seeking employment I was reluctant to put my address as "Salvation Army Hostel," so my Aunt Lily gave me permission to use her address No: 5 Pembroke Street, Port of Spain.  I secured a job as stock helper at Bata Shoe Company. My duties at Bata Shoe included labeling and packing shoe boxes.  After six months at the Hostel my aunt invited me to stay with her and have my evening meal. This enabled me to continue developing relationships within my family.  This aunt also assisted me with further education and my day work permitted me to continue studies in evening classes at the School of Business.

**Learning Business Practices**
My work gave me exposure to business practices and after six months I was promoted to stock keeper of over 2,000 items for the company.  The business additionally exposed me to purchasing and costing principles, production line experience and, in my capacity as a customs clerk for the company, I became aware of the international nature of business. After four years of hard work I was promoted to Assistant Purchasing Manager and also did production supervision for the company in the afternoon. I was fortunate to find favor in Port of Spain and became the youngest purchasing manager

at the manufacturing operation of Bata Shoe Company, Ltd. known as Trinidad Footware, Ltd.  This permitted me to have more interaction with foreign suppliers and the opportunity to learn more about purchasing procedures.  All of these experiences were preparation for my future.

### The Lesson from Volunteering

My supervisor and coach at Bata Shoe Company, Ltd was Mr. Dev Battachargie from India. He trained me in the principles of purchasing and costing.  He was most helpful and I learned a lot from his mentoring.  He owned a Volkswagen "bug" (PH 3918). Not having a car of my own, I volunteered to wash and clean his Volkswagen on weekends.  This I did each Saturday for about three years.  Mr. Battachargie was grateful for this volunteer service and when it was time for him to return to India, he called me into his office and gave me ownership of the car.  What a blessing! This was my first car and an appreciated gift.  Little did I know the menial work of washing and cleaning a car was sowing seeds for a blessing.  This experience taught me that volunteer work pays off in the end. Since then I have been encouraging others to do volunteer work.  **Just find something to do, and do it.  God keeps good records.** One never knows how God will take the energy invested in volunteer work and exchange that energy into a tangible benefit.  There is a blessing in just doing volunteer work.  I actually enjoyed washing and cleaning the little Volkswagen without knowing that someday it would be mine. I now better understand the sacred writing: **"and whatever you do, put your heart into it as if you were serving Christ your Master."** –Colossians 3:23 (DNT)

### Additional Training and Experience

Realizing the need for additional training in another area, a position as accounts clerk was accepted at the Singer Sewing Machine Company, Ltd.  This new job gave me valuable work experience and provided an opportunity to work and study

accounting with Mr. Herman Marcano, the financial comp-
troller of the company. This position provided opportunity to
continue my studies for the Accounts Executive Program. This
experience added to my foundational studies and allowed me
to grasp the common-sense principle that there are stages
in life that deal with **learning and reproducing.** After this I
moved ahead to Sampton Metal, Ltd., a subsidiary of Neal
& Massy, Ltd., as a purchasing and costing manager. I was
able to reproduce earlier common-sense lessons and practical business principles which produced good compensation
for my work.

**Words of Encouragement**
During my early employment I became ill with a kidney
ailment. During this illness it was at the Adventist hospital
in Trinidad that the Chaplain introduced me to the Bible. He
read words of encouragement and this gave me hope that I
would make it. When local treatment was unsuccessful, I was
sent to Toronto, Canada. My father sold a piece of property
to purchase the airfare and my uncle Emmanuel Persad, a
medical doctor in Canada, arranged treatment and provided
housing for me. My brother Bob who lived in Canada was able
to place me on his medical insurance which allowed me to
be admitted to the St. Michael's Hospital. I received the best
possible care and attention at this hospital. The operation
was a success; however, my badly damaged left kidney was
eventually removed. My brother was prepared to give me
a kidney if needed. **I was learning more about family and
divine intervention.**

**A Divine Intervention**
It was an intervention of God that provided the insurance,
the airfare, the doctors and the hospital which were part of
a higher power helping me understand that my work was not
finished. On my return to Trinidad I continued to work at Neal
& Massy, Ltd. and was then transferred to Cannings Foods,

Ltd. as a Route Sales Manager. This gave me much needed sales and branding experience.

## Following my Dream

Still following my dream to personally own a business, my accumulated work experience included stock helper, stock keeper, customs clearance, purchasing and costing, accounting and sales. Without fully understanding the process, it appears that a supernatural force had prepared me to move into personal business ventures in Trinidad and the United States. Not only did I continue to work hard, but now my thoughts were occupied with employees, assistants, buildings, products, production schedules and sales.

## Prepared for the Great Adventure

These opportunities of study and work in the business arena of Port of Spain further enhanced my experience and allowed me to grow and blossom where I was planted. This growth and development increased my desire to own my own business. Companies such as Bata Shoe Company, Ltd. and others probably never realized that God used them to prepare me for the great adventure now know as the Anapausis Partnership. I knew what I wanted to do, but the real issue was where to start and who was going to assist with the effort. So I decided to start in Trinidad where my family roots were. Surely out of seven brothers at least one would be willing to assist with new business ventures in Trinidad. At age 25 I started the House of Marketing, Ltd. in Trinidad.

## Youthful Struggle

**As a young girl** my Aunt Monica assisted my early education  which prepared me to go to work at age 16. My first work experience was an entry level office assistant at the law firm of Laurence, Narinesingh, Solicitors and Conveyancers. There learned the basic skills of secretarial service.

At that time in Trinidad and around the world, secretarial work was the door opener to advancement in many fields. This work taught me technical skills, afforded personal development, enhanced my ability to get along with people, produced dependability and helped me develop a team spirit. Once the technical and the personal service aspects of the task were mastered, these skills would lead me into another field of interest.

## Loss of a Grandfather

My memories of my grandfather are vivid and valued. He passed away when I was 19. This was my first experience of significant loss. His death was most painful and distressing and I cried until no more tears would come, but time gradually healed most of the wound. A strong memory of my grandfather's love for his family lives on and the pain of his loss lingers. The lesson of loss was hard to learn.

## Exposed to the Game of Tennis

During my early work experience, I was exposed to the game of tennis. There were tennis courts nearby and on the way home I observed the excitement and teamwork required in tennis. These were some of the same things I was learning in the office assistance and secretarial work. With my interest peaked in the game, I managed with meager funds to purchase a tennis racket. It was a handmade wooden racket with real cat-gut webbing. Surely it was fashioned by hand from a single piece of wood and the webbing cost the life of some animal to provide the webbing. This added to the worth and value of the tennis racket. I knew about the loss of life from working with my father's birds.

## Cost Associated with Benefiting Others

I learned that life has a balance and that the loss of one may be a gain for another. I had been raised around my father's birds and the family had often eaten pigeon meat. I was aware of the cost of life for the benefit of others. In reality the true value of some things are hard to fathom. For example, my tennis racket cost more than money. There was the wood that had been bent, twisted, and shaped by hand into the single handle for the oval tennis racket. Also this wood was special wood from a particular seedling that had to be planted, tended and harvested, to have the particular wood for an authentic tennis racket. There were many lessons from tennis.

**Lessons from Tennis**
First, there was the cost and value added to the racket from past experience and knowledge of its parts, then lessons came from the scoring, especially the strange use of the word "love" and "deuce" and of course the "numbers" used in ways that did not conform to normal arithmetic. There were lessons from the net and boundary lines that produced an awareness of limitations of personal movements. There were sides, singles, doubles, partners, contests, conflicts, wins and losses. Each of these fostered common-sense lessons that became beneficial to my growth and development and prepared me for a life of teamwork and cooperation.

**Equipped with Skills and Common sense**
Armed with secretarial skills and additional common-sense lessons from life and tennis, I was ready to take a further step into the world of business. My next employer was McEnearney Business Machines, Ltd. With this company my previously gained knowledge and experience were used to learn more about the machines of business and other aspects of trade and commerce. This was more preparation to move to another place of work and to learn even more to advance my career as a single woman.

**More Lessons Learned**
My next move was as a one person office manager with

Trinair, Ltd., an aviation company with thirty pilots and flight and cargo contracts. More lessons were learned about cooperation, coordination, contracts and contacts. My skills and shrewdness in business and personal relations were growing. Gradually I was getting ready to move up the ladder in the corporate world. The needed strength to climb the ladder came from the sales field. Selling safety and engineering supplies, industrial cleaners, and several upscale beverages was my next step. Learning sales, distribution, and initiating and marketing new products were the final pieces in my business development.

## My Fascination with Airplanes

Out of all my jobs in Trinidad I remember enjoying the one with the airplanes most. Airplanes fascinated me and I always wanted to fly. Perhaps this helped me decide to leave my homeland; at least I could fly and see the rest of the world I came to realize that there was much more to the world than Trinidad. Canada was the first stop, then on to New York for a while and finally to Washington, D.C. I worked in the National Capitol with the Australian Embassy for ten years.

## A Coveted Position

The embassy job was a coveted position and others desired the post. Receiving assistance from a few friends and perhaps some special favor from above made me grateful for this opportunity. Working with the Australian government meant meeting people from all over the world and I loved them all. My growing adult years were spent in Washington, D.C. I was involved in work and sports more than academics. My passion during these years in the District of Columbia was mountain climbing and cross-country biking. Occasionally my love of aviation was indulged by going to the National Airport near the Potomac River and watching the airplanes take off and land. Perhaps I was a little homesick or just wanted to travel more.

## A Longing for a Better Future

Somehow knowing I would someday meet someone who had a similar childhood and comparable youthful struggles as my upbringing, my hope for the future was developing. Knowing that struggles produced common-sense lessons and practical principles, I began to hope for a better and broader future and began thinking of returning to Trinidad. Today I realize that returning to my homeland was part of the plan for my life. Now those lessons are working for me and my mate in socially sensitive non-profit ventures and in profitable business ventures. God's plans are wonderful.

## Destined to Meet

Growing up apart in Trinidad but sharing similar lessons and principles for life surely I was destined to meet Subesh Ramjattan and become his partner in life, business, and service to others. Based on our childhood and youthful struggles, we were both committed to change the future of the children and young people within our sphere of influence for the better. Somehow a plan came together in both our minds that became evident years later. It was a plan as simple as **A.B.C.** and **1.2.3.** The business plan that would fund the charity projects and the social programs required hard work and sacrifice of time and energy. To fulfill the noble mission and our joint vision for our homeland we needed divine assistance as well as the support and partnership of individuals and stakeholders in corporations in Trinidad and Tobago.

What was this sophisticated plan that was as simple as **A. B. C.** and as easy as **1. 2. 3.**?

**1.** <u>A</u>ffection for children and families;
**2.** <u>B</u>usiness based on faith-based principles;
**3.** <u>C</u>ontacts to build a resource network.

**Transferable Principles**

The common-sense lessons that became faith-based principles we use to create programs, to construct buildings, and to change the hopes and dreams of disadvantaged children and dysfunctional families are transferable and could be reproduced around the world to make a difference in the lives of children, young people and family life anywhere they are applied with energy and persistence.

What was this uncomplicated plan that used cooperation and teamwork to accomplish so much to benefit children and family life? It was simple and straight forward: **work hard to make money and use the wealth wisely to fund projects for the needy.** The second thought: **the disadvantaged need more than money; they need affection and the presence of people who care.**

**The Personal Touch Required**

Actual hands-on human involvement and the personal touch are required to reach the heart of most social problems There must be no absentee landlords, but on-site participation in each project with a true demonstration of care and concern for those in need. The stakeholders must be visible and a genuine sense of volunteerism demonstrated by all who participate in ongoing projects. Most importantly the lessons Subesh and I learned in childhood and through youthful struggles were utilized to strengthen our vision for the future and make our life's mission both feasible and sustainable.

**Lessons we learned from Youthful Struggles**

❖ Armed with the practical skills learned from the family, the young can venture into the world of work.
❖ Family members should always encourage the enterprise of the young.
❖ Early discipline and study provide the courage to persevere in the adult world.

❖ Encouragement at home is a strong motivation for the young to venture into the larger world.

❖ Learning to live within the means of the family is the essence of morality in life and business.

❖ Learning never to take advantage of others is the first lesson in maturity.

❖ Early work experience teaches the young to bloom where they are planted.

❖ Learning that life has stages that include learning and doing is essential to a productive life.

❖ Learning to accept the assistance of family members is a good lesson.

❖ Each successful task moves one up the ladder of achievement.

❖ The mastering of the skills in one job prepares one for a better position.

❖ The lessons learned from extended family and early work will add value to the whole of life and prepare one for the difficulties that come in the adult years.

❖ Facing the reality of death early in life prepares one for the limitations of time and energy.

❖ Life and work have many unexpected lessons that prepare one for the next phase of the journey.

❖ Each common-sense lesson prepares the young for a life of teamwork and cooperation.

❖ Armed with practical childhood lessons young people are ready to take a forward step into the adult world.

❖ Developing a passion for the beauty of nature brings balance to life.

❖ Affection for children and families is the key to doing God's work.

❖ Using faith-based principles in life and business is a way to assure God's blessings.

❖ Developing contacts is the best way to develop a resource network to complete the mission and fulfill our vision for the homeland.

THE LOVE GATE

# CHAPTER THREE

## *ADVENTURES IN BUSINESS*

"Look beyond the challenges of broken lives to the
potential for a better life."

Ω

"Write the vision; make it plain."

Ω

"No one, including the poor and needy, cares how much
you know until you can convince them of
how much you care."

Ω

"Normally we do not use the word "success" because
it suggests more than enough; one can never do more
than is needed."

Ω

"God's work done God's way never lacks God's supply."

Ω

"If you release what is in your hands for God, then He will
release what is in His hands for you."

Ω

"Take care of God's business and God will take care of
your business."

Ω

**"God blesses you to be a blessing to others."**

Ω

**"Invest in people, property and poverty, the increase in value is worthy of both the effort and has a good return on the investment."**

Ω

**"There is a good reward for hard work especially when the bottom line is to assist the less fortunate."**

Ω

**"Give to support the ministry of others, but realize that your personal talents are needed to produce constructive projects to serve the needy."**

Ω

**"God put us together not only to help each other, but to work together for the good of others.**

Ω

**"Hard work is required to access the funds God provides."**

Ω

**"Bypass greed and give back to the need."**

Ω

**"A workaholic temperament could be an advantage to Kingdom building."**

Ω

## Foundation Stones for Business

Honest business practice started with my father's admonition, "Never steal from anyone." Mother's rule"16 ounces is 16 ounces" was added to the openness and integrity of my basic business practice. I tried to teach those who worked with me to **"Under promise and over deliver."** Also, I wanted those who worked with me in business to understand that an honest day's work deserved honest pay. Hopefully, the workers would catch the spirit of giving and sharing and understand that **one cannot give what he does not have.** Hard work then became a means not only to support myself and my family, but it provided the means to assist others. If the vision to assist needy children and work for the common good of families were to be accomplished, there had to be resources. Being a businessman my first thought was to use my business skills to generate funds to do the Lord's work. Then I realized that I needed partners to come alongside and assist with the task of funding the special projects.

## First Steps in Private Business

I started installing carpets and acoustical ceilings on evenings and weekends in addition to my regular work. My weekend and evening jobs together with my regular work were getting too much for me and it was necessary to make a decision to continue my regular job or quit and go out on my own. I decided to meet with my supervisor at the time and he determined that my evening and weekend jobs were earning more money, so he encouraged me to make the decision to move into the world of private enterprise. Early common-sense lessons and principles of openness and transparency helped me to make the right decision.

## The House of Marketing, Ltd. in Trinidad

The work experience and the educational opportunities in Port of Spain gave me sufficient confidence to formally start my own business in Trinidad in 1974 called the House of Marketing, Ltd. I purchased a used van from a previous employer and started installing carpets and acoustical ceilings. Then I hired contractors and started building a team of workers to complete all the contractual arrangements with customers. Materials were purchased from local suppliers until the company built sufficient capacity to import container loads from foreign suppliers.

## A Major Supplier of Building Materials

The House of Marketing, Ltd. became a major supplier of building materials operating with three branches. The company's operation is now approaching its fortieth year of operation and continues to provide support funding for various non-profit enterprises. The company not only sold materials but also trained many local professionals and thus increased the business and import capacity. The House of Marketing, Ltd. gained international recognition and reputation which allowed foreign suppliers during the downturn/recession of the 1980's to provide products to markets in the Caribbean. This opened a new door for a Miami, Florida, based warehouse and the past experiences in shipping and customs clearance became useful to the company.

## A Hiace Pick-up TP 724

My previous employer sold me the old vehicle I was using, a Hiace pick-up truck TP 724. After two months in my business I was approached for employment by Mr. Alson Stanley Jollie, a truck driver from my previous work place. He was my first employee. I always tried to build good relations with those who worked with me. I welcomed this new worker and former colleague to join me. I was getting my feet wet in the business world and now was seeing how good relationships with co-workers paid off in the future. All the lessons from previous business practices were now assisting my personal business venture.

## Favor with Local Suppliers

I started purchasing materials locally with very little money and found favor with local suppliers. I operated from my garage in a little house I built at # 13 Jordan Terrace, St. Augustine, on a lot purchased in 1973 for TT$3,000. My main source of financing came from deposits from customers. It was difficult in the early days of private business but after a few major jobs, credibility with my customers was gained and things got better. My basic common sense learned in childhood and my early employment were being translated into business principles. The one which became a foundation principle for my business enterprises was **"Under promise and over deliver."**

## A Big Step Forward

Business was growing and I had to put all my experience to work and exercise many of the lessons and principles previously learned. A big step forward came when I was approached by a local manufacturer to market his products. Office space and a partner were needed. I attracted a local partner in business with the idea that "two are better than one." My partner (now deceased) knew someone who had an office space on #139 Edward Street, Port-of-Spain. This gentleman allowed me and my business partner to share a 12 X 12 space. We had one secretary who was loyal and committed to the business. When I required the space for a meeting my partner would go outside and vice-versa. We worked together as a team and the business expanded and even attracted a foreign agency with iron and steel products. My preparation in the world of work was now being put to the test. We took little salary just enough to get by and started importing materials by securing a credit line/overdraft at the bank.

## New Product Line

The growing business needed more office and warehouse space. After two years we moved to the corner of Duke and Stone Streets, Port of Spain. We now opened a small showroom and a large garage became the warehouse. Carpets and ceiling materials were stored at the new location and we were able to house one of our foreign agents who sent a U.K representative in house to train us in their product line and to market their products on a commission basis selling directly to the customers. This was a new venture in Indent Sales. For Indent Sales, you sell and draw up two documents and the shipper sends the product directly to the customer and the seller gets a commission.

## A Venture in Commission Sales

The commission sales area was new for me and I learned

from this venture. I lived in the East and commuting to Port-of-Spain was a challenge. We trained sales persons, office staff, and we were now able to have our individual telephones installed – we shared a telephone in the past with the gentleman who shared his office space with us. Making international calls was impossible at times. We would have to place a call with the overseas operator and sometimes wait 4-6 hours before they would connect with the foreign operator. I sometimes had to travel to other islands that had easy access to international calling to do my business calls. We also relied on telex and telegrams for communication with our international suppliers.

### A Trincity Warehouse
We leased a warehouse in the Trincity Industrial Estate area and were able to purchase the building within three years. My warehouse and stock keeping experience was valuable for this operation. I was beginning to appreciate the lessons and principles learned previously. The parent company was **The House of Marketing Limited, Ltd.** My role was mainly purchasing, marketing, and warehousing products and my partner assumed the roles of administration, accounting and finance. The business was expanded into several associate lines. There were other divisions and each division had a manager. Those divisions were:

- **The House of Marketing Interiors**
- **The House of Marketing Partitions**
- **The House of Marketing Engineering**
- **The House of Marketing Commission Sales**
- **The House of Marketing Electronics**

### The Economic Downturn
The business expanded rapidly until the early 1980's when the economy of most of the world went through a recession including Trinidad and Tobago. Many owners of local businesses were selling out their properties and migrating to

the United States and Canada. During the economic downturn we managed to obtain a bargain on a property at the corner of Roberts and Alfredo Streets, Woodbrook, Port of Spain. This property was renovated into offices and the downstairs was used as a standby warehouse. At this time the business concentrated on building renovations and repairs to keep afloat financially. We survived the downturn of the 1980's by offering key managers the option to purchase the division they managed and operated. They realized that "a little piece of the pie is better than none at all," and they exercised this option and continued to make a living for their families.

During this economic downturn, I moved temporarily to the United States. During this period my children, Michelle and Nigel, came to attend school in the United States and it was when my daughter was enrolled in Dade Christian School on NW 67th Avenue and Palmetto Expressway that my life began to change for the better. My daughter's attending this school was the beginning of a change in attitude and lifestyle. This move was primarily for my children, but the move had divine consequences. God was arranging my life so I could come to know Him more intimately and be prepared for the final stages of work and service to the needy of my homeland.

**MINI Enterprises, Inc.**
The businessman in me could not stay still for long. I started a trading company from my home in Miami called MINI Enterprises Inc, named after my children MI-Michelle and NI-Nigel. I wanted to keep it small and manageable so the name MINI was a perfect fit. I used the services of Freight Forwarders to warehouse and load my containers to Trinidad. This was an excellent training school for my sixteen year old daughter to serve as my assistant. Since an apple tree does not bear grapes or as some say "the chip does not fall far from the block," my daughter would accompany me on buying trips and trade shows. Michelle gained valuable business lessons

and this was a good opportunity to share my life lessons and business principles. She also developed her own lines and made a larger business out of MINI Enterprises, Inc.

## Step of Faith
It was time to step out in faith since there were many bulk purchasing opportunities that were being offered to us. My carpet manufacturer offered me an opportunity as an Authorized Agent to represent their products. The work was growing and getting too much for us so we attracted a partner to assist with the export program. This new partner had great experience on the local market in the United States and we began to sell in three counties in Florida: Dade, Broward and Palm Beach.

## Georgia and Caribbean Partnerships
Developing a Georgia partnership, purchasing tufting machines, and developing a market for the new line of carpet with the bright colors desired by the Caribbean opened new avenues for business growth. Learning of a carpet finisher in Jamaica with excess capacity, the carpet made in Georgia was sent to Jamaica for backing and then distribution to other parts of the Caribbean. By completing the carpet process in Jamaica the product qualified for Caricom exemptions. With this advantage we were able to approach the Caribbean Common Market Customers. This operation grew and we partnered with a local mill in Georgia to manufacture Federal-Housing-Authority-approved products and distributed them in Florida. With company operated trucks on the road, next day service to these areas was offered. The process of taking distressed thread/yarn and making it into a marketable product was a good lesson learned.

## Open Connections
These experiences in International Trading have opened connections with International Bankers and Financiers. The

businesses were doing well and things seemed to be moving at a rapid pace since the business was now operating in Trinidad and Tobago, Miami, Florida, and Chatsworth, Georgia. I began looking for new and creative ideas to manufacture competitive products both for the local and export market. In my travels to Dalton, Georgia, the capital of the carpet world, I became aware of some opportunities. Introduced to the process of taking distressed yarn and converting it into a marketable carpet product, I entered into a contractural arrangement with a carpet mill in Chatsworth, Georgia to manufacture products suitable for the Sub F.H.A market in the United States and for the low end export markets.

## A Carpet Sales and Export

With this opportunity I initiated a carpet sales and export enterprise which also served the Caribbean region. My volume increased and this provided the confidence to purchase my own tufting machines and lease them to a small manufacturer to produce my own line of carpets and rugs. I made colors suitable for the Caribbean and the tropics. Learning that distressed carpet yarn could be taken and utilized to make a usable product planted a seed in my life that needy children could be salvaged from their neglected and abused lifestyle and made into young men and women who would be useful to society and could become productive adults to work and raise families. A lesson that would play out in taking neglected, abandoned, and abused children and making them into productive citizens and parents was formed.

## A United States Based Company

I registered a United-States-based company called **Floor Covering Distributors, Inc.** not only to sell the products which we manufactured, but also other approved brand names for mills that did not have an export department. We became their export arm and entered into contractual arrangements to sell their products. We expanded our warehouse in the

United States since the business was growing rapidly. We now had two loading docks and separate receiving ramps. Manufacturers were knocking on our doors seeking to use us as distributors. We developed our export market to include the ABC (Aruba, Bonaire and Curacao), the Caribbean and Central and South America. It was necessary to employ bilingual staff to deal with the Spanish speaking customers and markets.

**Burning the Candle on Both Ends**
Life was hectic, the pace was fast and the competition was getting fierce. It was starting to take a toll on health and family. I felt lonely inside because something was missing. I did not have peace of mind. I was consumed with business. My focus was on making money and more money. My life became confused, my candle was literally burning on both ends and I could hardly see daylight.

**Using Available Space**
Purchasing for other dealers in Trinidad with less than container loads, I was able to use the available space to ship other saleable items to create a cash flow for the company. I also partnered with a businessman in the southern area of Trinidad and Tobago to market and distribute products.

**Other Business Enterprises in the United States**
MINI Enterprises, Inc.
Southern Caribbean Shipping, Inc
Floor Covering Distributors, Inc.

**Other Business Ventures in Trinidad**
The House of Marketing, Ltd.
Drapery Land
The House of Marketing (San F'Do), Ltd.

**Learning the Secondary Mortgage Market**
During my routine exercise physical work-out at the Miami Lakes Gym, I connected with Mr. Juan Tony Cosculleula

who remains a friend until today. He introduced me to the Secondary Mortgage market business. Tony trained me in this new field and I was able to broker real estate and offer mortgage financing through his company for a commission. This added to my business proficiency and provided new experience in the US market. This friendship with Tony and the Cosculleula family has blossomed. He and his family are supporters of the work at Bridge of Hope. They have all visited Trinidad and Tobago and the project at the children's home.

THE LOVE GATE

# CHAPTER FOUR

## *CHANGES IN LIFESTYLE AND BUSINESS PRACTICES*

### Changes in Lifestyle

"Two are better than one for they have a good reward
for their labor"
Ω
"God put us together not only to help each other, but to work
together for the good of others.
Ω
"A God-fearing wife means a faith-partner."
Ω
"Live a life larger than yourself and work together with God in
the areas of the greatest need."
Ω
"Never look at a half full glass; see it filled, half with something
and half with air.  Then come to the knowledge that God is
spirit and fills the whole world and that the balance of a half-
full glass is filled with the spirit and presence of God."
Ω
"Your spouse is a gift from God."
Ω

**"God never wastes a hurt."**
Ω
**"Grow and blossom where you are planted."**
Ω
**"God, show me where your cause needs me most,"**
Ω
**"God is a God of 'another chance' not just a second chance."**
Ω
**"God calls us to be faithful, not successful."**
Ω
**"It is not go and do, but do as you go; in reality it is work
in your own environment, in your Jerusalem."**
Ω

## God Got My Attention
Change often comes slowly in life. In some cases there is drastic change in lifestyle and behavior, but in others a seed is planted, watered, and cultivated before it comes to fruition. It appears that this is the way spiritual matters entered into my daily life.  The seeds of truth were planted deep in my subconscious, but it took my illness with kidney failure to water that seed and open my eyes to see how Providence used the illness, family, doctors and hospital staff to get my attention directed toward the value of life and to think about the future.  Serious illness is one way God got my attention and helped me see my need to change and to value partnering with others to make life more effective.

## A Seed of Truth
As a young student in my village, teachers from the Presbyterian School began sowing seeds of truth from scripture into my life. At age 23 and during a serious illness I was hospitalized with a failing kidney. An Adventist hospital chaplain came to my room and read from the Bible words of encouragement that gave me hope in the midst of despair.  Although I was aware of the Holy Bible I had never been this close to death and had never listened with the same intensity as I did from a sick

bed. A small spiritual seed was planted in my life that would flourish later. The medical treatments were failing to solve the problem and there had to be additional intervention.

## Watering the Seed

Looking back on my life I can see how God used my illness, my family, and good medical services to spare my life for his work. Although I did not understand these facts at the time, the process was teaching me that a Higher Power was intervening in my life. When the medical treatment in Trinidad failed to produce recovery and the health issues became complicated, I was transported to Canada for additional medical treatment. With no medical insurance the concern was how could a gravely ill village boy find the resources for life-saving medical treatment in a foreign country? Providence intervened. My father sold a piece of property for my airfare to Canada. My older brother placed me on his Canadian Blue Cross/Blue Shield Insurance policy, and an uncle who was a Canadian physician arranged and supervised my treatment. Looking back it is easy to see how God had planned to care for me. God was getting my attention as a crucially ill young man. The watering of the seed of truth was in full operation. Providence was working and the watered seed was sprouting. Normally one who is dangerously ill and facing death would begin to look to a Higher Power for assistance, especially when family, friends, and the medical staff have done all they can do. This is what happened to me. When I was yet unsaved, God was caring for me and preparing me for his work.

## Cultivating the Tender Plant

With ice packs on my feet to contain the swelling and my body filled with intervention drugs, I arrived in Canada with little hope for a productive future or a future at all. The knowledge that the medical science of my homeland was unable to fix the diseased kidney was disconcerting. The fact that I needed drastic surgery and the prospect of a transplant to save my life created anxious moments in my young mind. God was still cultivating the tender heart. With the promise that my brother would donate a replacement kidney if it were required, small moments of hope began to develop. The watered seed was taking hold and I began to develop an expectation that I would recover and return to Trinidad, my family and to my work.

**The Operation was Successful**
After the diseased kidney was removed, I was welcomed into my uncle and auntie's home in Canada for a recovery period before returning to Trinidad. When I did return, my dream of owning my own business was uppermost in my mind. **My life had been spared for a purpose.** Exactly what that purpose was to be was not yet known to me. The only thing I knew was hard work so I put my mind and limited resources into starting the House of Marketing, Ltd. a business that still flourishes today and assists with funding support for the "anapausis vision."

**Can God Use a Workaholic?**
My workaholic mindset drove me to work hard to generate resources. I was determined to make my businesses work. However, this compulsive need to work hard for long hours took a toll on my health and my family life. I decided to take my children to Miami for schooling while I traveled back and forth between Trinidad and the United States. I had an upscale home in Miami Lakes, Florida, with a beautifully landscaped backyard and a pool, but something was missing in my life. God was permitting human circumstances beyond my complete control to alter my life and future. I learned later that God does not waste a hurt but with each and every difficulty brings a way forward. Each crisis in life is both a danger and an opportunity. A danger that I would become negative and miss the opportunity was a real possibility, but my better angels prevailed. When my children joined me from Trinidad, things began to change for the better. The needs

of growing children normally bring out the best in parents. My daughter was enrolled in a Day School operated by a local church and we began attending Sunday services and encountered people with a joyful attitude. God was working in my life.

## A Tender Plant was Growing

God again began to water the seed planted as a child, during the major health crisis, and from providential circumstances through the years. On Parents Day we attended the sponsoring church and I was surprised to receive benefit from the service. A few Sundays latter I made a profession of faith and began to make more time in my schedule for the children and my new faith. I attended a New Believers study class that led to water baptism. The tender plant was growing. My life was slowly changing for the better. God had been working on me; now I was working on myself. It seems that God opens the door, but we must have the courage to walk through the love gate when it swings open wide.

## An Eventful Journey

Attending a Christian Businessmen's meeting I was surprised at how happy the men were. I began to see a more pleasant side of life and my tender faith became strengthened. Providence had planted a seed of truth from the Bible, watered the seed with the kindness of family and friends, cultivated the tender plant with friendly and helpful medical staff, nourished the early growth during a recuperation period, and strengthened a young believer through adversity and Bible study. Without clearly understanding what God had done, I was beginning an eventful journey from the House of Marketing, Ltd. to the Bridge of Hope. My concern for the needy was beginning to take shape and the sparks of the flame that later became the "anapausis vision" was beginning to burn in my heart. I did not fully understand, but I knew clearly that something good was about to happen in my life.

## Chaotic Days and Restless Nights

Before a chaotic workday, I contemplated my future seated on the porch of my home near Miami. At the time, I owned seven businesses—three in Miami and four in Trinidad and Tobago, the southernmost island nation in the Caribbean Sea. I worked 15-hour days just to keep up with the demands. The stress made it difficult to sleep without medication. After one restless night, I began to think about how my life could be changed. I had seen Christian business people going through difficult times maintain a pleasant disposition. This brought a discovery that the faith-based principles they used could be applied to my life and business. This was personally encouraging. My drive to make money became altered and I began to move in the direction of assisting the poor and my love for God started to grow.

## Things Had to Change

Once touched by the hand of God, things had to change for the better. Moving from visiting bars to spiritual fellowship, my life seemed to take a new direction as I allowed God to become a reality in my life. Biblical studies became part of my daily routine and I started following faith-based principles from individuals who had used them on their life journey. My predisposition to act began to change and I made new and better friends who constantly encouraged me. The old Friday evenings at the bars changed to a time of spiritual fellowship and study with the truest of friends.

## A Difficult Time

During this period I maintained my business in Trinidad and this allowed me to spend time with my parents, Rosie and Dipnarine (better known as Pompie) who lived in the peaceful countryside. The sudden and unexpected death of my younger brother and business manager in Trinidad was a difficult time and happened when I was facing other life challenges. My new found faith and spiritual relationship with

God enabled me to face these tragedies with an upbeat spirit and a determination to continue my progress toward making my business profitable. God was tugging at my heart to be concerned for the needs of my native land.

**Seeking to be Debt Free**

I prayed and asked God to set me free of debt by age 50 and made a covenant that if this were achieved I would give my full energy into His service. During this time of transition an American missionary couple with a local pastor came to buy carpet. "I only came to buy carpet" became a chapter in his book called <u>After the Glory.</u> The gentleman was seeking a discount and wanted to see the owner. He introduced himself as Dr. Robert Doorn and his wife Dr. Glenyce Doorn and together with the local pastor he shared a bit of his life as a missionary for over 45 years and the "Story of the Glory in the Nations." They were known and called fondly as Papa and Mama Doorn. As a new believer I was prompted to ask them to be my spiritual mentors. As I write this book the relationship with this spiritual couple has strengthened over the last 15 years and has truly been a spiritual blessing.

**Watered the Gospel Seed**

During these years they have watered the gospel seed and encouraged me and my wife in the Lord's work. Papa and Mama Doorn have dedicated many of our projects. After many years of tutoring and guidance by Papa and Mama Doorn, both Debbie and I were commissioned into ministry on my 50th birthday January 25, 2001 in order to assist with the transition from business to a more fruitful time in serving others. Although business ventures must continue to support the projects, more time is now spent in serving the common good of children and families. Drs. Robert and Glenyce Doorn of Kingsway Fellowship International have become two of our mentors and accountability partners and we are privileged to refer to them as our spiritual parents. Their ministry skills and missionary zeal, together with their experience serving the needs of children around the world,  continue to be an asset to our lives and work.

## Seeking Guidance

During times of seeking guidance an urgent call was felt to assist the less fortunate on the eastern seaboard of Trinidad. I realized that God was guiding me back to my old hometown area of Plum Mitan.  There had been a conscious avoidance of the poor and the less fortunate, but a passion began to grow in my heart for the needy of my homeland. I had prayed, "Lord show me where your cause needs me most" and his answer was Trinidad and Tobago.  In my quiet time with God one morning these words came clearly to me as if someone was speaking to my heart:

> **"My son, my son, know that I am aware of your struggles,**
> **but be not afraid; for I will give you my peace,**
> **my grace and my love.  Be not afraid my son**
> **—for you will give direction to a lost people.**
> **Be not afraid my son for**
> **I will empower you."**

These words have been a guiding force in my life since that morning.  Each time I remember them, speak them, or write them the episode becomes real again and I am encouraged to keep pushing ahead.  Come grow with me; the best is yet to be.

## A Precious Gift

Good things do come to those who wait. I celebrated my birthday on January 25, 1994 and on the next day Debra Frost entered my life.  Debbie was to become my helpmate and partner on the journey to assist our homeland.  On Christmas Day, 1994 I received a precious gift and a life partner with my marriage to Debra Frost.  Debbie became a true partner and companion in my spiritual journey to assist the children and families of our homeland. God was still equipping and urging me forward toward a new and better lifestyle and a more unselfish view of business.

### Working Partners with God

Could it be the common-sense lessons and the practical business practices that we learned in the villages of Trinidad, in the youthful struggles, and in our early work experience prepared Debbie and me to meet the necessary criteria God had for spiritual companionship and faith-based partnership? Could it be that we grew and developed in the same soil and learned compatible lessons and common business practices to become working partners with God in the adventures called the Bridge of Hope and the Anapausis Partnership? We have come to believe this to be true and many who know us are beginning to see that the teamwork and relationship that have developed out of our common-sense lessons and faith-based principles were more than accidental; it was part of God's grand design to develop two individuals who together could produce the "anapausis vision."

### Adjustment and Challenges

All growth requires change and the marriage relationship is a close and intimate one between two human beings. The familiarity that marriage brings to a relationship may at times produce friction, but that is when prayer and faith-based thinking work to produce a better and more productive relationship. Much as an oyster with a grain of sand in its shell would cover the irritation with a pearl-like solution and make a pearl, each marriage has its own string of pearls that demonstrates perseverance and patience. With most marriages, adjustments and challenges are faced during the first years of marriage. As our relationship matured we came to understand that **God does not waste a hurt**, but often turns difficulties into lessons learned. These spiritual lessons advance the relationship journey along the path of faith.   Adversity often leads to advancement and loss becomes gain. A lesson learned that can be applied to most achievements is often repeated in many areas of life: **"No gain without pain."**

## Introduced to FamilyLife

We were introduced to FamilyLife materials and principles. The first one was defeating selfishness which caused us to examine ourselves, and the others were easier to work through.   These materials encouraged us to get involved in FamilyLife, a ministry of Campus Crusade for Christ.  We were blessed to visit Jamaica for training and then to Little Rock, Arkansas, for speaker training at the FamilyLife Headquarters. This experience allowed us to network with other couples and we even had the privilege to critique professional FamilyLife speakers at a major conference in Little Rock with over 200 couples.   FamilyLife offers a series of life building products and programs. Home Builders are interactive sessions where couples meet at a couple's home and together discuss the principles of marriage.   Valuable lessons are learned so couples do not have to enter either human or spiritual battles without ammunition.  A marriage mate is not an enemy but is a gift from God.  Since God does not make junk, couples must learn to value each other.  Debbie and I learned a good lesson that made a difference in our lives.

## A Prayer and Faith Partner

Finally, I had a prayer and faith partner. When two agree before the Lord on a direction, powerful things can happen. Partners become accountable to each other and true companions on the journey toward spiritual fulfillment.  We have come to realize that marriage is a contractual relationship in which each one must give up something to gain something even better.  Could this kind of spiritual partnership be a fulfillment of a statement in the journal of a young missionary killed by the Auca Indians in Ecuador many years ago: **"A man is no**

**fool who gives up what he cannot keep to gain what he cannot lose?"**

### Love Changes the Attitude and Lifestyle

The love was mutual and as the relationship grew the vision and mission were expanded. We started pursuing the things of God together and began to see more clearly our purpose and calling in life. Even the earning of money had a lofty purpose and was somehow connected to the vision. We began to seek divine strategies to clear debts and restructure the business enterprises in Trinidad. True love changes the attitude, the predisposition to act, and a new and better lifestyle comes from a committed relationship. Working together with God is a good place to be in life and work. We learned from Scripture in Amos 3:3 that there must be agreement for two to walk together in harmony. This kind of spiritual unity and togetherness enabled us to walk in harmony. This teamwork made the journey worthwhile and productive.

### Guidelines for a Love Relationship

We want our marriage to be a model for others and especially for the children; therefore, we try to follow a principled life and set an example. The solemn pledge represented in the marriage vows are general guidelines for behavior of both spouses. Our spiritual life has brought faith-based principles into our marriage relationship. In the Torah (Law of Moses) there are over 600 behavioral guidelines that were used in ancient times to assist the human family. Below is a paraphrasing of the original Ten Commandments that had a male orientation. The guidelines for marriage are based directly on these commandments but are not gender specific. Marriage principles and responsibilities relate to both parties relative to acceptable behavior to maintain personal integrity and moral uprightness in the marriage relationship. These practical statements are based on the intent of the

Ten Commandments and are good guidelines for a working marriage.

1  You must have no one else but me.
2  You must not keep mementos from past romances.
3  You must not worship any strange gods.
4  You must respect my name and my family.
5  You must both work and worship.
6  You must respect and support your parents.
7  You must not harbor hate for anyone.
8  You must not adulterate the marriage vows.
9  You must always tell the truth about our neighbors.
10 You must not desire a house beyond your means, or covet anything that belongs to your neighbor, including the neighbor's spouse.

## Changes in Business Practices

"Write the vision; make it plain."
Ω
"Take care of God's business and God will take care of your business."
Ω
"God blesses you to be a blessing to others."
Ω
"Lead by example in every aspect of both personal and professional life."
Ω
"Invest in people, property and poverty, the increase in value is worthy of the effort and has a good return on the investment."
Ω
"Your influence is positive when you are a good example in all aspects of life."

**"Money cannot purchase happiness, but it can pay the bills."**

Ω

**"Every person one meets regardless of his or her station in life can add something worthwhile to one's knowledge and experience."**

Ω

**"There is a good reward for hard work, especially when the bottom line is to assist the less fortunate."**

Ω

**"Give to support the ministry of others, but realize that your personal talents are needed to produce constructive projects to serve the needy."**

Ω

**"A workaholic temperament could be an advantage to Kingdom building."**

Ω

**"If you release what is in your hands for God, then He will release what is in His hands for you."**

## A New Start in Trinidad

It was now time for a new start in Trinidad. New management was hired for the House of Marketing, Ltd. and the business was expanded into other areas. The loss of my brother and business partner was a heavy burden I could not carry alone. I came to a decision to dispose of assets and business in the United States so I could return to my homeland and my primary business to save the "goose that laid the golden egg." These changes required many adjustments to my life, but I was thankful for divine intervention in my life. I soon came to the realization that my **Heavenly Father does not give his children a burden they cannot carry and with every difficulty God provides a way forward.**

Much energy and long hours of hard work were necessary to overcome the challenges at the House of Marketing, Ltd., but our prayer life was working. Things were changing for the better. It was understood that prayer was not just getting the answer from God, but trusting and partnering with God with confidence that guidance for the journey was from above. The ancient words of St. Paul dealt with the present issue:

> **1. As we work together with God, we appeal to you not to accept the grace of God and let it go to waste. 2. (God said, I have heard your prayers at a  convenient time, and in the day of salvation I have brought you relief in a difficult situation: observe, now is the time for coming together; now is the day of deliverance.)**
> —2 Corinthians 6:1-2 (DNT)

## Make the Vision Plain

I diagramed on a piece of paper my seven businesses, following the ancient words from Habakkuk 2:2: **"Write the vision; make it plain"** (ESV).  Sensing the need to simplify, I sold my businesses in Miami and Trinidad, except for one: The House of Marketing, Ltd. a lumber and plywood business which I started as a young man of 25. I felt comfortable with my prayer partner and friend, someone to whom I am accountable and I love deeply; Debbie is also my "Bouncing Ball" with ideas and things that bother me. As our relationship grew and blossomed, the vision and mission expanded.  We started pursuing the things of God together and began to see more clearly our purpose and calling in life.   This is a question constantly asked **"Is our life rightly related to God and can we expect Him to manifest His blessings in our lives?"** It helps to keep us in check and in right alignment with God's plan. The earning of money had a purpose and was somehow connected to the vision.  We began to seek divine strategies to clear debts and restructure the business enterprise in Trinidad and the USA.

A few week later a sales manager Mr. David Duncan from a local company came to visit with me to sell his products. After our discussions, he said to me that this was a good business and if I had any intentions of selling at anytime to please let him know.  I then said to him, "What about now?" Within three months the sale was concluded - God again preparing the way. A separate company was established for the sale of the business except for the lumber and plywood division. Since this part of the business was not profitable at the time I could not sell it. We retained the assets of the Lumber and Plywood Division and a new corporation was formed called the House of Marketing (Trincity) Ltd. and sold this new entity to Mr. Duncan.

## A Way to Replicate the Vision
Following the changes in attitude and lifestyle, came an understanding that my business endeavors were part of Kingdom business and were to be operated for the glory of God and in turn to benefit those in need. Business had to be more than just the bottom line. Money was important, but I came to understand that how it was earned and how it was used were more important. Not only could I provide jobs and onsite training for young people to learn the common-sense lessons that I had learned growing up, but they could also be exposed to the faith-based principle that were guiding my business operations. In this I saw a way to replicate my vision and instill dreams of better times for those willing to work.

# The House of Marketing Limited

"UNLESS THE LORD BUILDS THE HOUSE, THE BUILDERS LABOUR IN VAIN"
PSALM 127:1

## A Kingdom Business
My business was now a Kingdom business used for the glory of God. **"Unless the Lord builds the house, the builders labour in vain."** (Psalm 127:1) This is the Psalm we chose to have painted on our warehouse. To God is all the glory!

**God-sent Mentors**

Several God-sent mentors assisted me along this spiritual journey to a new way of life. I began to feel the need to give back and share with others the blessings I had received. I was troubled by the thought "How can I ever pay back the good and blessings I have received?" Gradually I understood that I did not have to pay back; God's blessings and family and true friends did not expect anything in return for their assistance. Then I came to understand it was not a pay back at all but a kind of pay forward as I invested in various projects to serve the needy. I came to realize the best way to pay back was to assist others on their journey. A passion for the poor developed that had been purposely avoided, and it became a kind of obsession and even an excitement to become involved in a project to help the disadvantaged. A simple prayer became routine in the daily devotions: "Lord continue to show me where I am needed the most."

During these times of seeking God, an urgent call was felt to return to the less fortunate on the eastern seaboard of Trinidad and Tobago. I was being sent back to my hometown area. This provided the time and opportunity to strengthen my relationship with my parents and to "give back" the honor and assistance they deserved from a loving son. Now I was in the right place and it was the right time to meet new partners.

**No Time to Waste**

The death of Debbie's grandfather when she was young and the sudden death of my younger brother and business partner taught us both that a higher power controls one's time on earth. This suggested that one does not have time to waste and all work must be done quickly and without hesitation, because life is short. Also, we learned that a great loss can open doors of opportunity to a different and perhaps an even better future. The way one deals with loss speaks of character; character being an internal motivation to do what is right. One must be careful not to allow their ability to take them to a place or position where their integrity could be compromised.

## Adversity Leads to Advancement

One old adage about life stated **"It is not what happens but what one does with what happens that makes the difference."** A saying attributed to Napoleon about the struggle of battle is appropriate here, **"There is a time in every battle when both sides have lost — victory belongs to the one who attacks first after this point of loss."** The lesson here is clear; when trouble comes, one must take positive action to move past the difficulty. Often difficulties are open doors of opportunity.

It was important for Debbie and me to talk but also to walk and practice the talk. The lessons we learned from the struggles of married life and the events that made our marriage special particularly the principles of resolving conflict and learning to communicate with each other were valuable. Laying aside the things that would hold us back and pushing forward toward the goal became important. We made an agreement that we would not both be angry at the same time. A statement attributed to U.S. President Truman was helpful, "It is understanding that gives us the ability to have peace. When we understand the other person's viewpoint and they understand ours, then we can sit down and work out our differences."

## Lyrics of the National Anthem of Trinidad and Tobago

Forged from the Love of Liberty in the
Fires of Hope and Prayer.
With boundless faith in our destiny
We solemnly declare;
Side by Side we stand
Islands of the blue Caribbean Sea.
This our native land
We pledge our lives to thee.
Here every creed and race finds an equal place.
And may God bless our nation.

THE LOVE GATE

# CHAPTER FIVE

## *DECISION TO ASSIST THE HOMELAND*

**"The state of a nation is not judged by the infrastructure and buildings but by the prevalent attitude toward infants, children, families and the less fortunate."**

Ω

**"Without developing the children into moral and honorable citizens, there will be no viable state."**

Ω

**"The future of children in Trinidad and Tobago is in our hands."**

Ω

### A Solemn Pledge

With the current words of the National Anthem on our minds and the sacred words of ancient scriptures in our hearts, we solemnly pledge allegiance both to God and to our nation. We will devote our health, wealth, wisdom, and work ethic to making Trinidad and Tobago and the larger Caribbean region, and the world a better place to live, work, worship, and bring up a family in the fear and admonition of the Creator. With confidence in our fellowmen and hope in our hearts, we pledge our sacred honor, our honest trust and our treasured ideals to the needs of this nation. So help us God!

### Allocating Funds

We started building homes using my experience and expertise

in the central part of Trinidad. Before the houses were completed, they were sold. We allocated part of the profit into a
separate account which would be to start our God-given ministry when He was ready. We completed approximately 12
houses in two years and accumulated about sixty thousand
dollars in this fund – awaiting God's call – we were ready.
**"You cannot give someone something you don't have."** We
had our house in order, ready and waiting on God's call. My
simple prayer was still **"Lord show me where your cause
needs me most."**

### A Stake in the Outcome
We understood that prayer was not only getting the answer
from God, but trusting God and partnering with God regardless
of the outcome. However, I understood that one must have a
stake in the outcome of prayer to pray sincerely. Much energy
and long hours of hard work were necessary to overcome
the challenges at the House of Marketing Ltd.; we had to put
our backs against the wall and fight a good fight, laying aside
every weight and running with patience the race before us.
Focusing on a goal greater than distractions along the way,
we developed endurance in the process: inward strength to
withstand stress and endeavor to do our best.

### Servant Leadership
I learned about servant leadership and understood that
it meant to lead by good example and also to serve my
customers and workers. I started to build a new team of
leadership. It was about relationship building since **rules and
regulations without relationship – lead to rebellion.** I met
with my key staff and allowed them to share their personal
financial statements with me since it was my desire to see
them be successful and to gain from the process, proceeds
and profits of the business.

## Loyalty of Staff

I remember meeting with a delivery truck driver, Mr. Satnarine Nanlal whom I knew from the country village of Plum Mitan. I looked at his diligence and gave him the opportunity to join the staff team. His brown delivery truck TAG 1277 needed repairs and it was a good time for him to sell the truck and take the money and put a down payment on a property since he was renting at the time. He started learning to use the computer, and I also spent time in mentoring him. Today he is our operations manager and doing extremely well for himself and his family. He owns his home and drives an air-conditioned SUV. His commitment along with the loyalty of my secretary, Zobida, and staff allows me to spend time pursuing the spiritual side of my commitment, which I call the **things of God.**

## Planning was Crucial

We considered three reasons for planning. (1) First we had to take a **long-range look at the future** of our homeland. Unless this was done, we could not fulfill the second part of our plan, (2) **to take advantage of opportunities.** What became obvious to us was the need of neglected children. They needed care and education, medical assistance, and some desperately needed a decent and safe place to live and grow. We saw many dysfunctional families and young people without purpose. We also saw a great need for the common-sense lessons we had learned and the faith-based principles we were beginning to practice. The task was great and we knew that we must have a clear vision of what needed to be done and a practical mission to accomplish this goal. We came to understand that what we do for ourselves dies with us, but what we do for others will become our legacy.

We knew we could not do it alone and must take advantage of each and every opportunity to secure partners to advance this plan. We did not want to get bogged down in problem solving and believed that many problems are solved by time and energy (money). Most strategic developers do not permit either time or money to hinder a worthy project. To get things done...things must be done! In strategic planning, problems that developed in a previous project are solved in planning the next endeavor; therefore, only when a project was nearing completion would we consider dealing with the third part of our plan, (3) **deal with problems.** We wanted to use each opportunity to assist with solving the problems of the needy, but we knew this would take time and funds and that working partners would be needed to fulfill our mission as a collaborative enterprise.

## Using Opportunities to Solve Problems

Many problems are solved through using the opportunities that current circumstances present. Problems can usually be solved by asking questions: What can be done better for the next project? What can be done differently the next time? What can be done new for the next project that will make it work better? **Experience is the best teacher.** There is always room for improvement. Problems do not develop in a short space of time but are normally the result of long-standing neglect, failure to do something that was needed. Often it takes as long to solve a problem as it took to create the difficulty in the first place. We knew if we worked too much in the problem areas many of the things would not be accomplished. The concentration was to design and construct facilities, create programs, and bring individuals into these facilities and programs as a means to an end. We also knew that many of the problems in a society require some faith-based assistance and life-changing conduct to make a difference. With the help of partners and divine assistance, we believe a difference can be made in the lives and circumstance of the needy. Hebrews 13:16 (DNT) records "You must remember to do good to others and give alms; God takes pleasure in the sacrifice of gifts."

## Problems on the Back Burner

I returned from the United States to Trinidad to use my wealth, wisdom, and newly found strength in worship to benefit my homeland. When I met Debbie, she partnered with me in the venture to assist the homeland. Teamwork was the founding principle that guided our future planning to care for needy children as a foundational step to improving family life in our homeland. The process of looking to the future of Trinidad and Tobago provided unlimited opportunities for service. In the process of taking advantage of opportunities, various needs were uncovered and plans developed to solve individual, family, community, and national problems. Opportunities were the open door and the Love Gate was the passage through which Debbie and I walked together to serve others. Problems could wait or be solved in the process of constructive change. Our new attitude was Educational Opportunities.

## Multipurpose Campus

**Campus Crusade for Christ** came aboard early in the Anapausis venture and is housed on the compound with all their programs for schools, churches, and families, most specifically the programs of FamilyLife. The **OASIS UNIVERSITY** was initiated in 2002 and is housed on the Anapausis compound, to offer masters level courses in FamilyLife Education, Organizational Leadership, Educational Testing and Measurements, and doctoral studies for the social professions: clergy, doctors, lawyers, NGO leadership, businessmen, church groups, teachers, social workers, childcare providers, and the list goes on and on.

The University is under the Accreditation Council of Trinidad and Tobago (ACTT) and is an alliance partner with Oxford Graduate School for doctoral studies; however, two programs leading to a Doctor of Ministry and a Doctorate in Educational Leadership designed specifically for the Caribbean are in the works for the local campus. The emphasis is on training men and women to serve in Trinidad and Tobago and the Caribbean region. The studies are interdisciplinary and culturally specific to the Caribbean to bring about an integration of the professions and disciplines to produce constructive social change in Trinidad and Tobago and the larger Caribbean region.

**The International Children's Academy for Neuro-development (I CAN)** is a project for children and adults with specific needs are housed in newly constructed facilities on the Anapausis Compound to serve all those who need such services. Various academic conferences and workshops are sponsored and held on the Anapausis compound to advance various aspects of education and social change for the region.

(I CAN) is a new project which joined the Anapausis campus in Curepe to serve the children of Trinidad and Tobago. The leaders of the I CAN approach to development, shared with me that Neurodevelopment has given both assistance and hope to those with learning, speaking, hearing, focusing, and memory or mobility challenges. It has also helped others considered "normal" or "advanced" to release their learning potential.

The brain develops in an orderly, sequential manner. Behavior/function is a result of the brain receiving information, processing it, storing it and giving an output. Any impediments at any of these stages will lead to inappropriate function. When the basic brain development is delayed or disorganized, a person will struggle to learn, focus or sit still, follow directions or clearly understand the consequences and social cues. However, the brain can change (due to its plasticity) with specific stimulation done with consistent frequency, intensity and duration. These stimulations assist in organizing the brain and creating new neural connections thereby improving brain efficiency, function and behavior. If a person's brain is properly organized, one can move forward to an advanced level of learning and development.

The Neurodevelopmental techniques utilize an exclusive developmental profile to evaluate individual functional levels in vision, hearing, language, manual and motor skills, and other associated areas. An individualized specific stimulation and educational program is then designed to accelerate and improve the physical, mental, developmental, cognitive and emotional needs to the next level and beyond.

Neurodevelopment training addresses "how" the brain learns to acquire the ability to learn and adapt to the everyday environment. This training focuses on increasing and improving the functional brain systems that produce the ability to learn, attend, remember, interpret feelings and sensations, coordinate and apply reasoning ability. The most common underlying cause of daily frustrations can be found when the brain is not efficiently organized to allow functional brain systems to naturally work together.

**Caribbean Psycho-educational Assessment Services, Ltd.**
On the Anapausis campus a facility has been created to perform psycho-educational evaluations and assessment services. The leader of this project shared with me that  it offers a wide range of educational services regardless of age or stage of development.  Children, youth and adults may be tested, treated or referred for treatment.  There are complete diagnostics, prescriptive reports, and follow-up services provided for gifted children, slow learners or dyslexic children. Learning, language and behavior disorders are part of the services.  All services are provided by competent and academically certified professionals.

## Change Agents

Debbie and I wanted to be not only catalysts to produce social change, but we wanted God to change us in the process and help us become change agents that are participants, not just observers. The difference in being a catalyst that is not altered in the process of causing change and being a change agent, is that people involved in producing the change are themselves altered in the process of helping others. With the religious transformation which came to our lives, there are not only changes in business practices and lifestyle; as projects are developed to assist others, our determination and excitement are also growing about future programs to assist the needy of our homeland.

## The Basic Difference

A failure to understand the basic difference between a catalyst and a change agent is to fail to see the real change that must take place when working with the disadvantaged or the needy. It is easy to become calloused and overlook the poverty that is so pervasive around us. Both a catalyst and a change agent have the same objective – producing change in others, but a change agent is also changed in the process. There can be no true change in the social fabric of the community unless those precipitating the change are also changed as part of the ongoing progression. Compassion and concern must grow and multiply to meet the growing need. It must be evident to all who support projects that the participants are changed for the better and are truly sensitive to the needs of the community. Change can be a wonderful gift. It is the key that unlocks many doors to growth and creates excitement in organizations. Change is not easy, but is a necessary part of progress. My acrostic of D-O-O-R guides me in the process of dealing with change:

**D--ecision**
**O--pportunity**
**O--bedience**
**R--elationship**

## A Mutually Interactive Process

It is this mutually interactive process and responsive behavior that makes for constructive social change in areas of benevolence and compassion to assist the less fortunate. This is how we want to apply the strengths of the Anapausis vision and bring such projects as Bridge of Hope to bear on individual and community needs. Projects are planned, designed, visualized, promoted, funded, evaluated and completed in time to start the next project. In project development a strong effort is made to remember the needs for which the project was developed. The desire to serve the needs is the driving force that completes the project, initiates and continues the operation to serve others. This is how charities and socially responsible organizations and individuals develop over time to become more involved in the needs of a community.

## There was a Two-Track Plan

First the common-sense lessons learned in childhood and early work experience had to be translated into business practices to create a more responsible business resource. Then business entities had to be reorganized to produce more funds to provide the extra funding for the special needs projects. This not only included making existing business ventures more productive, but also the developing of new entities to produce funds for projects.

Being unable to consider the next step was unacceptable for me, so foundational principles were executed to guide the choice of the next business venture or the next charity project. Providing state of the art planning and accounting and applying the learned principles, the next phase of the journey became obvious and possible. Providing stakeholders with an overview of the process and the progress produced cooperation in future ventures. In all projects and business operations I try to be transparent and use both the long-range view of the finished project and observe the day-to-day progress to ensure it is following the stated plan. This dual-track process is the normal operating procedure for my endeavors.

## The Long-Range Perspective

The Long-range view works backward from a perception of where the project is going. Such a plan is used in construction when a builder views both an architect drawing of a completed building and a set of working drawings of how the building is to be constructed. The builder, with a clear view of both plans and a conception of the finished product, establishes a target dates for each stage of the development. The objective is to complete a project without waste and within budget.

Working back from the target date, the builder considers time, material, and contingencies to establish a construction schedule. At this point the builder must start at the beginning, structure the building in stages, and arrange for an evaluation process based on the architect's plans and the budget. Each aspect of the project must be done in sequence with the time line affected by the duration of each stage. With such a plan the builder may evaluate progress using some kind of daily report system to determine the next step. When such an advance plan is followed and the budget constraints considered, there can be sustainable development in the charitable sector of community projects and program development.

## Planning and Oversight

Each aspect of a project is viewed in the light of prerequisites. As each stage is satisfactorily completed, the project moves to the subsequent stage until the project is completed. Without a planned timeline, the performance evaluation cannot remain on schedule. The clock is running on each project. Certain things must be done within specific time frames or the opportunity passes and may never return. This requires both planning and oversight of projects. This is a big part of the transparency in my operation. I want stakeholders to fully understand each step of a project so they can be assured that funds and time are used efficiently.

## Investment of Resources

We felt the need to invest resources to assist the less

fortunate children of Trinidad and Tobago. In March of 1998 an opportunity came to take over an existing children's home. There were twenty-five needy children in the home and the challenge to look after them was accepted, but more help was needed. We visited Plum Mitan, the village where I grew up, and found a family of six abandoned children. The eldest was a 12-year old girl and the youngest was just two years old. These abandoned children were living with the bare necessities with no running water or lights in a wooden house on stilts with rotted and missing floor boards. The children had not had a bath in months and suffered from scabies, a skin disease. This was an eye-opener since we were not adequately equipped to deal with medical and health issues at this new operation we called the House of Young Christians. We were able to convince a couple from the village, Anderson and Esther Joseph to fill the position as House Parents. They served the organization for ten years. Esther has now proceeded to be trained in Adolescent Development Programs with Servol and became a teacher at Servol.

**Developmental Pathway Plan**
When the custodial facility is working with needy children, a Developmental Pathway Plan is prepared for each child. This includes medical evaluation, understanding their background and former environment, assessing their education and developmental level, and testing or evaluating each child for any deficiency which might be repairable. The developmental pathway will ultimately lead to an endgame or a period of transition from custodial care to the real world. **This is the final and greatest challenge of custodial care.** Partners are constantly needed in this effort.

A camp facility was built and named after my nephew, David, from Canada, and a Canadian group partnered with us to assist the children at Camp David. Groups would come during their spring and summer breaks and share their time and talents teaching the children and the community. This project was successful and the concept assisted in engaging the community in the childcare project. The desire to assist the children in this place was rapidly growing beyond the financial resources and the available facility. New children were admitted to the home and the childcare project was out-growing the available space. We began to search for a new sight to build a new facility to become a model for custodial care. It would be called the Bridge of Hope.

## A Safe and Stable Place

A new five acre site was located and purchased where a safe and stable place could be constructed to fulfill the vision. Because of several factors and hard lessons learned, the name of the childcare project was given a new name: **Bridge of Hope.** The word "bridge" was used to express divine or spiritual intervention in the lives of needy children and the word "hope" suggested a remedial healing of the past disappointments and negative experiences of the children plus the promise of a better future. It was clear that we could not "put new wine into old bottles." Abandoned children who come from neglected or abused backgrounds needed a safe place to heal and grow, to be loved and educated and equipped for a productive life. With the help of God and a few individual and corporate partners the work on the new facility was initiated.

---

### SEEDS OF HOPE

Bridge of Hope has been in operation along the Eastern seaboard of Trinidad changing standards of living since 1998. As part of its community outreach program, Bridge of Hope and the Kernahan Community have partnered with BPTT, COCAL Estate and SERVOL, in initiating the Kernahan Centre for Community Development (KCCD). This project is in an effort to address some of the needs in that community. Our pioneer programs at the centre have been a Preschool, Video Production Training for youths, Parent Outreach Programs and Adult Literacy Classes.

---

**Vision for the Bridge of Hope**
The vision for Bridge of Hope included a capacity not only for basic childcare, but also residential quarters for the children with shared bathrooms not communal facilities, a pre-school, special education school, an images skills program, a multi-purpose hall, quarters for staff, dining facilities, playground, common areas and special training space. The project attracted the attention of Mr. Clive Pantin and the FEEL organization that came alongside to assist us and the vision for Children's Villages of Trinidad and Tobago was birthed. Achievements attract attention, and when a project does well, it recommends itself to would be supporters. A vision is more caught than taught. The total budget for the new project was in excess of five million TT dollars or about 850,000 USD.

Such a project cannot be completed by one or two; many corporate and private citizens came alongside us. The Board of Directors, including the Chairman, Mr. Jewan Ramcharitar and Mr. Satish Paraigh, a Director, came up with a strategy that we should challenge individuals and companies to cover the cost of a child's room. They were the first to support this plan and other directors and private citizens came alongside and enough funds were raised to complete the project in 12 months.

The House of Marketing, Ltd. invested a sizeable amount by faith even though the funds were not available at the time of the pledge. With full confidence that God would provide, the company increased sales by 25% with only a small increase in expenses and the pledge was covered without any frustration. The key principle is simple, **"When you take care of God's business, He will take care of yours."** One should never be afraid to step out in faith and do what God calls or impresses should be done.

**A Seed You Sow**
Dr. Glenyce Doorn taught us a key principle: **"Your giving to God is not a debt you owe, but a seed you sow!"** One should sow seeds on fertile ground. The achievements of Bridge of Hope have created "fertile ground" and attracted many corporate sponsors, including, Republic Bank Ltd., Royal Bank of Trinidad and Tobago, Ltd., Scotiabank, Citibank, Ferriera's Optical, Ltd., United Way Trinidad and Tobago, and United Way International. Many who have the vision for Bridge of Hope are grateful to the organizations and the individuals who came alongside the project and enthusiastically supported the goal of quality childcare for the disadvantaged children. By faith Bridge of Hope acquired the 18 acre tract behind the facility as a long-term investment. Local timber has been planted on this property to ensure sustainable development and long-term viability for the Bridge of Hope.

**Searching for a Partner**
In 2008 the Bridge of Hope enterprise was approached by a major company in Trinidad and Tobago (BPTT) searching for a partner to deliver a project in a poor rural area. Kernahan Village was suggested, a village similar to where I grew up. Kernahan is a village of about 150 families situated on the eastern seaboard of Trinidad and Tobago. A survey established a need for a school in the village.

It was reported by the Trinidad Guardian that education was not a priority. The village is a farming community. Many homes are built on swamp land and there is no running water. The Bridge of Hope challenged a major corporation, Cocal Retreat, Ltd., who owns land in the area, to donate ten thousand square feet for the construction of a school. The project was completed debt free and the preschool now operates with an enrollment of 25 students ages 3 to 5.

There are over 200 species of birds in the area of the Village of Kernahan and the area is known for eco-tourism. Seven teenagers in the area were engaged in a video communications program to make a video to highlight the strengths of the village and to bring an awareness of the village's value to the families. The plans include pursuing special education from this location for the families in the village. Operation plans also include a Computer/Homework Centre and an Image Skills Program. The Head Teacher of this school was once a childcare worker at Bridge of Hope. Bridge of Hope was the vehicle for her to pursue training for qualification in Early Childhood Education.

**Kernahan Centre for Community Development**
Children in the Village of Kernahan will no longer spend their days catching cascadura and just playing, but will start going to school in a new Community Centre building and learn to use their time wisely. Research by the Central Statistical Office showed that 35 children below age five were not attending pre-school. Although adults in the village work hard, they also were heavy drinkers and the village was plagued by a mixture of social problems. This is why the workers at Bridge of Hope extended a helping hand to this troubled community by constructing a school/community centre.

The press reported the Centre was a project of the Bridge of Hope, an NGO and included a pre-school. Cocal Retreat, Ltd., an estate in Manzanilla, provide the land for the project, and a Trinidad and Tobago Petroleum Company (BPTT) furnished the initial funding. Bridge of Hope managed the project and the initial operation. Servol furnished the teachers for the preschool. Other contributors were Chartwell Baptist Church (Canada), Agape Bible Ministries, Mayaro/Rio, Claro Regional Corporation, and Kernahan residents themselves.

# KERNAHAN CENTRE
## FOR COMMUNITY DEVELOPMENT

The Kernahan project was initiated in 2008 and completed in 2009. Bridge of Hope will be continuing as a partner in this project. The new centre is a multi-purpose facility and will be used by the community as an educational effort beginning with pre-school and also reaching adults through counseling and skills development programs. It will also contain a community library and a program to assist children with homework.

A primary objective is to lend a hand to single mothers and unemployed women and assist them with learning marketable skills. Bridge of Hope will support an adult literacy program and the Social Justice Group of Trinidad and Tobago will assist the marketable skills program with video and multi-media production. There will be an effort to stimulate eco-tourism in the Kernahan community.

A statement attributed to Mac Anderson and B. J. Gallagher points to the attitude those who serve must have:

**Life is not about waiting for the storm to pass; it's about learning to dance in the rain.**

### The Long View
The Anapausis Society is a legacy plan to gather and equip the brightest couples and leaders in Trinidad and Tobago including both couples and individuals to carry on the mission of the Anapausis partnership and the vision of Bridge of Hope. This is a plan to sustain the vision and maintain the completed projects. The Anapausis Society will seek to apply the anapausis vision and anapausis partnership mission to anticipated future events, developments, and opportunities. The desire is that our vision will become a calling for others who will attach special importance and devote special care to the mission of caring for the children and families of Trinidad and Tobago. The reader will find more data on the Anapausis Society in the PostScript at the end of the book.

## *Bridge of Hope Declaration*

Send your abandoned and neglected children,
The abused ones who ache for relief;
Across the bridge of hope through the love gate,
They will find a safe place to live and grow!

THE LOVE GATE

# CHAPTER SIX

## *CHILDCARE MOVES TO THE BRIDGE OF HOPE*

"Look beyond the challenges of broken lives to the
potential for a better life."

Ω

"No one including the poor and needy cares how much you
know until you can convince them of how much you care."

Ω

"God never wastes a hurt."

Ω

"God is a God of 'another chance' not just a second chance."

Ω

"Your influence is positive when you are a good example
in all aspects of life."

Ω

"Lead by example in every aspect of both
personal and professional life."

Ω

"Look around you, there are needy children in
close proximity to you."

Ω

"It has been said that a human being can live about 40 days
without food, four days without water, and four minutes without
air: but only a miserable life without hope."

**"Never be inconsistent in dealing with disadvantaged children, they have already witnessed sufficient discrepancy and contradiction in their previous environment."**

Ω

**"Live a life larger than yourself and work together with God in the areas of the greatest need."**

Ω

**"There is a good reward for hard work especially when the bottom line is to assist the less fortunate."**

Ω

**"Give to support the ministry of others, but realize that your personal talents are needed to produce constructive projects to serve the needy."**

Ω

**"Tithing and giving multiplies the nest egg and enables one to care for the needy."**

Ω

**"One should tithe both time and talent."**

Ω

**"Bypass greed and give back to the need."**

Ω

**"The future of children in Trinidad and Tobago is in our hands."**

Ω

**The gate to the Bridge of Hope childcare facility has been named "The Love Gate."** As each child enters the home and as each visitor walks into the compound where the children live, they will pass through "The Love Gate." A gate

THE LOVE GATE

is a doorway, an entrance, an opening, an opportunity, a new start, a new beginning. Love includes caring for, adoring, affection, friendship, devotion, and spiritual passion. This is exactly what we want the children who come to Bridge of Hope to experience. When children pass through the "love gate" and cross the Bridge of Hope, this journey will suggest many emotions and attitudes about a positive future. An acrostic of love might assist an understanding of the overall intent of the Bridge of Hope:

## L.O.V.E. is:

**<u>L</u>earning from the past.**
**<u>O</u>pening your heart to others.**
**<u>V</u>iewing life with confidence.**
**<u>E</u>njoying a hopeful future.**

## OBJECTIVES FOR A CHILDCARE FACILITY

1.  Create a home environment conducive to learning that promotes growth, mutual respect and trust among children and caregivers.

2.  Structure childcare programs to educate and develop children, giving priority to behavioral and learning needs of disadvantaged children.

3.  Provide structures, learning resources, technology and processes designed to motivate and engage children in learning activities and programs of development to prepare them for the real world of work and family.

4.  Develop a tutoring/learning process that permits self-directed, individualized, face-to-face, and classroom learning in real-life situations with dialogue/support systems and technology suitable for disadvantaged children.

5.  Strive for multicultural awareness with a broad exchange of teaching/learning experiences across cultural and ethnic boundaries.

6.  Partner with business and industry to produce meaningful programs for childcare and development in regions of need.

7.  Work with the Government and Child Protection Agencies to establish quality childcare facilities and train qualified childcare workers and staff.

**Opportunity Equals Obligation**

In 1998 an opportunity was presented to us to take over an existing children's home in the Eastern seaboard of Trinidad and Tobago. Since the overseer of that ministry was giving it up, we took up the challenge and founded the House of Young Christians, a custodial care facility and a home for abandoned, abused and neglected children of the area. God showed me where His cause needed me most. We clearly understood that opportunity brought with it an obligation. It is our firm belief that a core truth is **"The heart of God is family."** This is why God commands us **"to care for the widow and orphan."** The word orphan originally meant "fatherless" but has been expanded to include those neglected or abused who do not enjoy proper care from a structured family environment.

**Pure religion and undefiled before God and the Father is this, To visit the fatherless and widows in their affliction, and to keep himself unspotted from the world. --James1:27 KJV**

**Support for the Vision and Mission**

Debbie's background and life experiences caused her to be supportive of the mission to the poor, and this enhanced our relationship and increased our ability to accomplish the vision of helping disadvantaged children. Instead of doing this venture alone, Debbie joined me as a partner and working together made things easier. I learned that **"a burden shared is not as heavy."** Debbie's interest in fitness and nutrition began in her early teens when she became aware of the need for exercise and proper nutrition. She was certified as a Fitness and Nutrition Instructor in June, 1997. This became useful when we started the children's home and understood the children needed assistance in both of these areas. Most of the children were undernourished for both spiritual and physical nutrition. Debbie has applied her knowledge to assist the children in these areas. Their progress is measured from the time children are admitted to the home. Proper nutrition and physical fitness eliminates many childhood problems and enables them to focus on their everyday lives in a more positive manner.

In 1998 we formed the **House of Young Christians,** a custodial care facility and home for abandoned, abused, and neglected children in a needy area. "The House of Young Christians" was founded with the original intent of being a "boys' home." After meeting the first family of three boys and three girls, the Board decided to establish a home for boys and girls to better meet the growing need for custodial care.

## A Board of Directors for Bridge of Hope

A Senior Partner of PricewaterhouseCoopers – Mr. Jewan Ramcharitar accepted the role as Chairman of the Board, a post which he presently holds. His counsel and leadership role in the organization has been most beneficial to the ministry in allowing us to be transparent and accountable.

**Board of Directors**
Jewan Ramcharitar (Chairman)
Subesh Ramjattan (CEO)
Debra Frost-Ramjattan (Secretary)
Brian Vital, Rodney Ramjattan, Anil Ramdin,
Allan Saunders, Steve Mohammed and Satish Pariagh

**Auditors:** Aegis Business Solutions Ltd.

Jewan Ramcharitar immediately pulled a team of people together including several community activists and conducted a workshop in order to come up with a vision and strategy document. Our vision became very clear. **"to be a model children's home."** In March 1998 we engaged children from the home to participate in this workshop. This exercise allowed a greater understanding and acceptance of the vision and more participation by the community. The people of the community felt they now had a stake in the childcare project.

Debbie and I together lead the Board of Directors, and visit the home as often as possible. It is a great feeling to see the growth and development of the children. To remember where they were and how they appeared before coming to the home and seeing them laughing and playing is a wonderful feeling. We just wish that all those who support the vision could feel this sense of excitement and contentment in the children

**First Needy Children**
The first family to come to the home clearly demonstrated the need of some children. It was hard to believe that six children were living and sleeping in one bedroom. The tragic truth is that there are more needy children than the capacity of custodial care in Trinidad and Tobago. We have built a model home but Bridge of Hope can only care for a few compared to the many in need. The prayerful concern of the public is needed. **The future of the nation depends on how we meet this need.**

It was necessary to quarantine these children for a period of one month before they could function normally in the home with the other children. The nature of the case with these six children was a cause that had to be taken to the community. We immediately engaged the people of the community in the project, because we felt the community was a major factor, as to both cause and cure of the problems with the children.

It was felt that the community must be aware of the neglected children and begin to play a major role in the project. To involve the community, adult literacy and computer programs and other life skills instructions were offered that would assist the people to find ways and means to assist the neglected children.

**Several Projects**
Several ministries and projects were developed to benefit

children both individually and collectively with the ultimate goal of sustainability. The vision for the House of Young Christians developed into the larger mission of the Bridge of Hope with multiple services to needy children and the community. Looking at the causes of abused, abandoned, and neglected children produced a Family Life Ministry and the need for improvements in national education.

**Moved from a shack**

**to a home**

*The first Community Outreach project*

### Business was Consuming our Time

We wrestled with God about the business of the House of Marketing Ltd., since it was consuming our time. We prayed that God would send us a buyer for the business to allow us time to do His work and will. God gave me a strategy to advertise a sale of merchandise sitting in our warehouse for a long time – the sale was called "Grab It or Lose It." We advertised, the people came and we discounted the items below cost. "A little piece of the pie is better than none." We sold over 75% of the items that were dormant in the warehouse. This gave

me the ability to pay a huge sum to the bank and allowed me to operate with a clearer peace of mind.

## Transition to Bridge of Hope

We saw the hand of God in the transition from the House of Young Christians to the Bridge of Hope through the Love Gate. The home is certainly not a basket of bad apples that needed to be culled from society. It is filled with precious fruit of the womb picked prematurely from the tree of life to prevent deterioration and given special care to preserve them for a positive future. It is a happy place filled with the giggles and laughter of playing children and is designed to apply the medicine of laughter to the dry bones and broken spirit of disadvantaged children.

Bridge of Hope is a cradle of socialization where children

are assisted to gain skills required to function successfully in society. It is a place touched by the Hand of God for the benefit of abandoned, neglected, and abused children. The Bridge of Hope concept is what the words "bridge" and "hope" suggest to the children and to those who may support the project. Bridge of Hope is a connection, a link to the poor and needy children. It provides a passage out of poverty into a brighter future through care, education, and training. Bridges are used to cross troubled waters and dangerous places. A paraphrasing of a popular song speaks to the issue of a place that brings hope.

**Cross over the bridge and leave your troubles behind;**
**Honest affection and true compassion you will find.**
**Over the Bridge of Hope and through the love gate,**
**You will find a real home and family at last.**
–With apology to Benjamin and Weiss (1945)

Paul Simon wrote lyrics (1969) about providing comfort to a person in need and called it a "bridge over troubled waters." The original tune started as a modest Gospel hymn but became more dramatic as he collaborated with Garfunkel and others for the public performance (1970). Simon's lyrics were about a friend who was always there to help. The friend becomes the bridge over the troubled places in life. The last note of the production was on a violin, and was a long, drawn out E-flat that lasted ten seconds. With apology to lyrics of Simon and Garfunkel, hopefully the songs, harmony and the last note of the Bridge of Hope will be at least a sharp (a half step higher than the natural note rather than a flat note that is one half step lower.)

One goal of Bridge of Hope is always reach higher and higher and to point the children to the high road in life.

**When you have weariness and pain or feel small,**
**When tears run down like rain on a wall;**
**Cross the Bridge of Hope and we will dry them all.**
**When times are rough and friends are not around,**
**Like sunshine after a storm, friends can be found.**
**Walk over the bridge of hope through the love gate;**
**With open hearts and loving arms we patiently wait.**

We want the children of the Bridge of Hope to reach for the stars. Lofty goals and high ambition are needed to become a person of achievement in the real world of work. Hope springs eternal in the human heart and soul. Everyone seems to be in pursuit of happiness and hopes to find it somewhere on their journey.

Hope is a concept that requires two things **desire and expectancy.** Without both one has fear. Should one want something to happen, but did not believe it would happen; they are afraid it will not happen. If one believes something will happen but does not want or desire it to happen; they are fearful it will happen. So to have real, genuine, sincere hope one must have both a desire and faith. The Bridge of Hope is designed to instill hope for the future and confidence that the future will be better than the past. This removes fear and produces optimistic anticipation. In reality **H.O.P.E.** in terms of an acrostic is **H**elping **O**ther **P**eople **E**njoy – a better view of themselves and of their personal future.

Since complete and seamless love removes fear; consequently, the "love gate" at the Bridge of Hope produces hopeful anticipation that life will be better. Mature love with no patch work, no start and stopping, and is one continuous process that removes fear and produces hope.

**Love has no room for fear; and indeed, love drives out fear and when it is flawless love it drives out the punishment of fear;**
– I John 4:18 (DNT)

---Copy of painting by BartLGreen

Often on the days we visit Bridge of Hope, we would sit at a table in the spacious dining room of the children's home wearing bright colored T-shirts with the Bridge of Hope emblem. We would hear such things as:

"Uncle Subesh, look at me," says a young resident named Leo as he cartwheels across the dining room, his tiny frame bending in graceful arcs.

"Hey, that's pretty good," we say.

Then some child will say, "Auntie Debbie, look at me, I can do......"

This time of togetherness is great for all of us. We trust

that our marriage is a model to these children—many whose concept of family is shattered. Every time we visit the home, we are consumed by activity. Standing in the kitchen at the home in the midst of a busy day sometimes, I just put my arm on Debbie's shoulder and smile, and in my heart I say, **"You matter to me."** Working with disadvantaged children has taught us to value family and that time is precious. We believe that this is where doing great things for God begins.

### The Need for Workers who Care

The simple goals at Bridge of Hope for the childcare process are: (1) stimulate the interest of the child in life, living and growth; (2) arouse their spirit of inquiry about the world and the Creator, and (3) get the child talking and otherwise involved in the activities of the home. With this admonition: the caregiver must excite and direct the self-activity of the child and as a rule do nothing for them that they can do for themselves. Children in custodial care must be taught self-reliance and to do for themselves all things for which they are capable. Growth and development is in fact the process of action and discovery.

### The Language of the Heart

Individuals who feel an urge, desire, or call to work with children and especially those who want to work with abandoned, neglected, and abused children in the custodial arena must learn to speak the language of the heart. They must learn to listen and multiply their love. Love is something caregivers must never divide; it ought to be multiplied by the number of children in their care circle. Love is understood as T-I-M-E!

### Room to Grow

Bridge of Hope uses the skills of teachers and caregivers and the available space of a school to grow both body and spirit. The laughter of the children is priceless. When a visitor walks on the campus of Bridge of Hope, they find happy children.

They will see children playing, reading, studying, learning crafts, learning trades, learning to play music. We even have a "steel pan" band. The vision of the childcare program is comprehensive. We sow the seeds of hope and water each kernel until it begins to grow. We give the gift of hope to children who had almost no prospects in their previous environment. Bridge of Hope sends out News of Hope to supporters to keep them informed of the program, progress and the growing needs of the children.

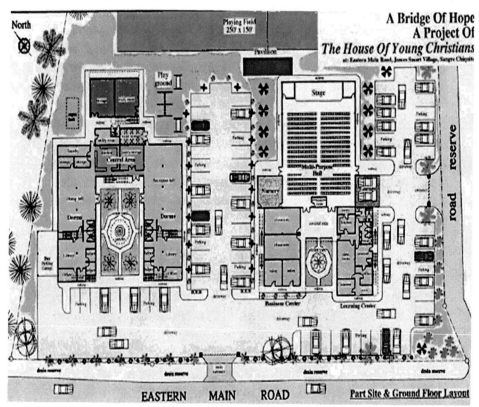

**Footprint of Bridge of Hope Campus and Compound**

### Committed and Volunteer Service Providers
A custodial care facility is a place of committed and volunteer service providers who supply the remedial training needed to

gain an age-specific level of development for needy children. The home is a happy place filled with the giggles and laughter of playing children and is designed to apply the medicine of laughter to the dry bones and broken spirit of disadvantaged children. There is a relationship between the attitude, knowledge, and behavior of caregivers and volunteers in remedial and surrogate parenting and quality custodial care for abandoned, neglected, or abused children. This is why we seek the best staff available in Trinidad and Tobago and then bring in extra individuals to do the special work of testing, evaluating, and assisting the staff with medical and behavioral problems of the children.

**A Positive Atmosphere**
Just how does a caregiver create an atmosphere conducive to remedial and productive development? There are several steps in this process if it is to influence both cognitive and affective development. We encourage everyone related to the Bridge of Hope to lead by example in every aspect of both personal and professional life. Children must never witness inconsistency in the caregiver. Children placed in custodial care have already seen sufficient discrepancy and contradiction in their previous environment. Influence will be positive when workers are a good example in all aspects of life

### Growth and Change

**Bridge of Hope Vision**
Bridge of Hope will be a model children's home that is known for being the best childcare provider in Trinidad and Tobago and the Caribbean and be a change agent for improving the standards of all other similar children's homes. We will be a centre for family life development and a satellite outreach for proven effective programs.

**Bridge of Hope Mission**
To bridge needs to opportunities for at-risk individuals, families, organizations, and communities that want partnering using approaches that:

- Provide a non-threatening environment
- Cater to real needs
- Build life skills
- Develop local change agents
- Promote stakeholders to own the vision and contribute charitably

**Bridge of Hope Values**
There are four primary values at the Bridge of Hope. We must be ethical in all activities. The goal is to empower the children for a better life. We want to be inclusive and never turn anyone away who needs assistance. Most of all we want to see good character development in each child to prepare them for the real world.

1. **Ethical** – good governance, management and transparency.
2. **Empowerment** – nurturing self-esteem and developing Bridge of Hope full human potential.
3. **Inclusive** – no one turned away because of race, gender, or religious beliefs.
4. **Character** – holistic character development.

**Bridge of Hope Current Programs for Community Outreach**
- Image Skills Program  (Australian Embassy and IADB)
- RBTT Community Reading Room
- Computer Literacy Classes (NESC & Ministry of Education)
- Preschool  (SERVOL & Petroleum Woman's Club))
- Special Education School  (Charis Works)
- Community Medical Centre (J & J Trinidad Ltd.)
- Community Playfield  (Republic Bank, Ltd.)

- Agriculture Project (Million Dollar Round Table
- Distribution of food baskets and clothing (various donors)
- Multi-Purpose Hall (FEEL—Foundation for the Enhancement and Enrichment in Life)
- Life at The Crossroads (FamilyLife and Citigroup)

**An Image Skills Centre**
In 2005 the Bridge of Hope together with the Inter-American Development Bank (IADB) established an Image Skills Centre (ISC) to provide youth in the neighboring communities with technical and on the job training in hairdressing and cosmetology. The decision to deliver a training program in beauty therapy was based on a survey of neighboring low income, rural communities to determine areas of interest for young women in particular. This program offered graduates a range of income generating opportunities, including self-employment or either part-time or full-time employment. Glenda Bhagwandass, a certified beauty therapist, donated her time and talents to this pilot program. As a result of this effort, eighteen young ladies from the community have graduated.

## *Operation Principles:*

**Trust**
**Reliability**
**Good Governance**
**Accountability / Transparency**
**Inclusion of Community / Stakeholders**
**Shared Vision / Strategy / Learning**
**Leader / Leadership**
**Sustainability**

***http://bridgeofhopett.org***

**A Partial View of the Campus at Bridge of Hope**

## For the Love of God

that we

### Subesh & Debbie Ramjattan

Do lay this foundation stone on the
25th day of January 2005

In service to the children and people
of this Great Nation.

Mark 10:45
**"For...the son of man...came to serve."**

*Love is seeing in others what Christ saw in them
when He created them."*

**This is recognition for the investment that
Subesh and Debra Ramjattan made in the Bridge of Hope.**

## Scope of Operation

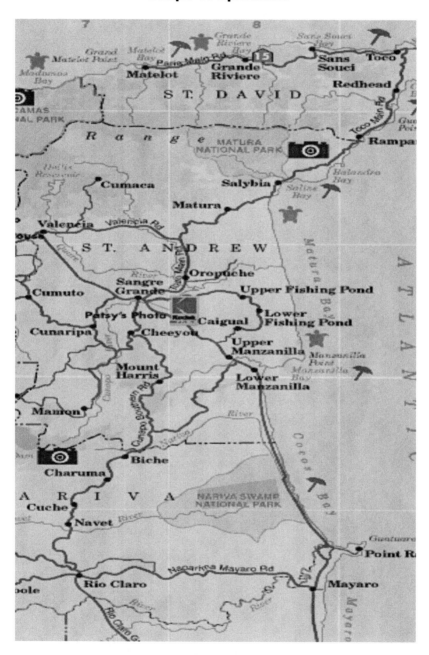

<u>http://bridgeofhopett.org</u>

THE LOVE GATE

# CHAPTER SEVEN

## *THE JOURNEY TO ANAPAUSIS*

"If you release what is in your hands for God, then He will release what is in His hands for you."

Ω

"God blesses you to be a blessing to others."

Ω

"God's work done God's way never lacks God's supply."

Ω

"Grow and blossom where you are planted."

Ω

"It is not go and do, but do as you go; in reality it is work in your own environment, in your Jerusalem."

Ω

"Never look at a half full glass; see it filled, half with something and half with air. Then come to the knowledge that God is spirit and fills the whole world and that the balance of a half-full glass is filled with the spirit and presence of God."

Ω

"Invest in people, property and poverty, the increase in value is worthy of the effort and has a good return on the investment."

Ω

"Live a life larger than yourself and work together with God in the areas of the greatest need."

Ω

"God put us together not only to help each other, but to work together for the good of others."

**Constructing the Anapausis Compound**
Having survived many adversities including the passing of my brother, and business challenges, we embarked on building a home in the Santa Margarita area. We moved into the home in March of 1996 and after 18 months a friend visited and offered a large profit if he could purchase the home. With no intentions of selling the home, an offered price that would totally free us from debt was tempting. After prayer and consideration and a call from Dallas, Texas offering three acres of property on Upper Mohammed Street, with reluctant but total agreement from Debbie, the decision was made to sell, settle debts, and build a new home.

**An Open Invitation to Utilize Anapausis**
In 2001 I had a divine encounter at the Center of Excellence, in Macoya, when I met Chancellor Hollis L. Green, ThD, PhD of Oxford Graduate School. Dr. Green greeted me by saying. **"Did God put you here to help me, or can I help you, or can we do something together?"** I shared with him that we were building a compound at Anapausis on Upper Mohammed Street and he should come and see if he could use it for his project. This meeting initiated the OASIS UNIVERSITY in Trinidad to serve the Caribbean region.

**O.A.S.I.S.** is an acrostic for **O**mega **A**dvanced **S**chool for **I**nterdisciplinary **S**tudies and offers several graduate programs and opportunities for doctoral studies. The goal is to train individuals to serve the Caribbean. The university and the academic programs are housed on the Anapausis compound and the academic program is approved by the Accrediting Commission of Trinidad and Tobago (ACTT). As Chairman of the Board I am pleased to have Dr. Green in retirement from Oxford now serve as Chancellor of OASIS UNIVERSITY. This institution of higher education is making a difference in Trinidad and Tobago and the Caribbean region. The University is well underway to becoming a major player in the educational environment of Trinidad and Tobago and the Caribbean region. OASIS is an Alliance Partner with Oxford Graduate School/ACRSS (American Centre for Religion and Society Studies) and the university is expanding the academic programs to better serve the Caribbean region.

## Anapausis Compound

The new place was to be called by a Greek word "anapausis" meaning "a place of refreshment." Pictures on the next page are: [1] Our new home called Anapausis; [2] chapel, now an apartment; [3] A 3-story conference centre including classrooms, dining, sleeping quarters, offices, and chapel, research library, and meeting rooms. [4] Other compound buildings house Campus Crusade for Christ for Trinidad and Tobago; [5] OASIS UNIVERSITY. [6] The International Children's Academy for Neurodevelopment (I CAN). {7} The Psycho-educational Assessment Services Ltd.

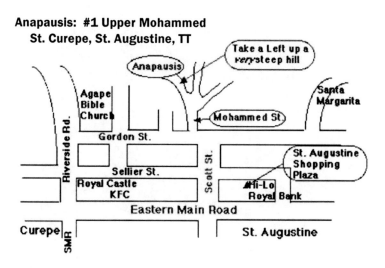

**Anapausis: #1 Upper Mohammed St. Curepe, St. Augustine, TT**

**1**

**2**

**3**

**4**

Be patient. Don't get in a hurry. It takes time to do great things. The delay of the full message caused discouragement. Don't worry; we may have already won the battle. God has the funds and the plans to meet the growing needs. When one possesses an aggressive will to win, the certainty of winning is multiplied many fold. It is important to hear the full message to gain the encouragement and celebrate the victory. We must not let the fog of indifference and neglect snatch defeat from victory. The viable future of those we have spent so much time and energy in rescuing from a disadvantaged environment depend on the transition plan. They must not be turned back into the same kind of environment that created their previous distress.

THE LOVE GATE

# CHAPTER EIGHT

## *SUPPORT AND NETWORKING*
## *WITH PARTNERS*

Based on our prayers and personal experience with God, the words of St. Paul speak directly to how we feel about working with God and others:

**1. As we work together with God, we appeal to you not to accept the grace of God and let it go to waste. 2. God said, I have heard your prayers at a convenient time, and in the day of salvation I have brought you relief in a difficult situation: observe, now is the time for coming together; now is the day of deliverance.**
–2 Corinthians 6:1-2 (DNT)

We see these faith-based principles directly applicable to our support and networking with partners:

**"Every person one meets regardless of his station in life can add something worthwhile to one's knowledge and experience."**
Ω
**"God, show me where your cause needs me most,"**
Ω
**"Write the vision; make it plain"**
Ω
**"God blesses you to be a blessing to others."**

"Invest in people, property and poverty, the increase in
value is worthy of the effort and has a good
return on the investment."

Ω

"The future of children in Trinidad and Tobago is in our hands."

Ω

"Live a life larger than yourself and work together with God in
the areas of the greatest need."

Ω

"God put us together not only to help each other, but to work
together for the good of others.

Ω

"Hard work is required to access the funds God provides."

Ω

"Tithing and giving multiplies the nest egg and enables
one to care for the needy."

Ω

"One should tithe both time and talent."

Ω

"Bypass greed and give back to the need."

# SUSTAINABILITY

### Sustainable Development

All projects must be sustainable. We will work to develop
buildings, infrastructure, and staff that can be maintained
with the promised level of support. The objective is to initiate
a project, develop a plan, construct the facilities, bring staff
aboard, receive the individuals targeted for assistance and
operate on a strict budget living within the means provided.
There will be an ongoing effort to network with stakeholders
and individuals who can continue the support required to
sustain the operation and remain effective in the planned
mission.

### The Redirection of Resources

A committed group of determined citizens can substantially

affect the redirection of resources to empower the poor and bring about positive social development that is sustainable. The word development is used because it is an advance, an increase, an enlargement, and improvement. Sustainable is used because of budget plans for multi-year operations, pledges over time, multi-year grants, annual support gifts, monthly faith promises, and corporate and government funding. Unless concern for the poor makes it from the subconscious into the heart and into the attitudes about lifestyle, **talk without the walk** will accomplish nothing. Teaching without acting is either mute or speaks so loudly in the negative that more harm than good is done. A good example is always the best policy.

### Green Money vs. Brown Money

In the fields of stewardship and fundraising there are two kinds of money: green and brown. Green money is recently earned money and the more recently it was earned the greener it is. Brown money is old money that was inherited or savings, or unearned income from stocks, bonds, or interest on deposits. Individuals have sweat equity in green money and the closer the money is to a pay check the more the sweat equity adds value to the currency.

### Sweat Equity

Individuals who work hard to earn money develop sweat equity in the currency. When they part with the funds they are giving of their expended energy. Volunteers or individuals who work at reduced wages for a faith-based organization are also developing sweat equity in the project. This sweat equity is as good as gold because those who have invested time, energy, and funds want to see the project flourish and grow. This is part of the assurance that the early work will not be in vain.

A hard working laborer who received pay on Friday for digging a ditch all week may give a small amount as a gift, but may feel as if he has done a great deal.  On the other hand, a person of wealth may make a large donation and feel that not much was given.  A gift is measured by what it costs the giver in effort and energy.  Corporate funds and money generated by a business are considered brown money.  Grant funds also fall into this classification.  Ask largely from such entities. Those who make the decisions to fund a project, whether a social endeavor or a charity event, normally do not have "sweat equity" in the funds they disburse.  Ask large.  Such entities can give without feeling the hurt.

**A Green Money Operation**
Normally nonprofit or faith-based entities need both green and brown money.  Brown money supports the infrastructure, buildings and equipment.  When individuals become volunteers or workers provide recently earned cash, they are both giving green money because of the sweat equity in the gift. They are delving into their living and time.  It is these funds that feed the children, buys the clothes, and cover the basic operation of the entity.  When stakeholders in corporations or individuals of wealth make generous contributions to a worthy project, they are normally giving to construct buildings, purchase furniture, and other big budget items.  This is considered brown money. Grant funding and large donations often come with a proviso of "matching funds," which means they will give you the money to build the building if the project planners will provide the necessary green money for daily operations.

Faith-based institutions operate on green money with weekly offerings and occasional gifts.  Institutions such as schools, childcare centers, and not-for-profit faith-based ventures need brown money to survive.  They do not have access to the common labor and weekly offerings, but must depend on a few persons of wealth who will share out of their "brown money bag" to support the program or cause. This does not exclude the small but regular gifts from working people. Both brown and green money are needed to make a project work.

Weekly operational funds may depend on green money from average people, but building projects, new programs, and charity causes must depend on brown money from a few persons of wealth. Ancient scripture was clear that one should "Ask large" when seeking to support a nonprofit venture. Scripture also says "God loves a cheerful giver." Brown money does not have the attached sweat equity value and may be given cheerfully because the gift does not cause pain. Those who live from paycheck to paycheck and work 40-hours each week to eke out a living place more value on the money with a sweat equity evaluation.

**Spiritual Equity**
Equity is the value placed on something over and above the actual monetary value. For example, a few dollars to an elderly person living on a social pension would be valued much higher than many times the same amount out of the wallet of a rich man. In fact when the widow gave a few coins in the Temple, Jesus observed the gifts of the wealthy and compared the value of the widow's gift and said, "Truly this poor widow has given more than everyone." Divine evaluation or one might say "spiritual equity" is based on what it costs the giver. God loves a cheerful giver and this adds spiritual equity to the value of the gift. This means even the smallest gifts from a sincere person may be more valuable than you noted. It is firmly believed that "spiritual equity" can stretch the budgets of not-for-profit and faith-based enterprises. Never despise the day of small things. Great oaks grow from small acorns.

**Social Guilt**
In every community there are wealthy individuals who store up funds and close their eyes to the needs of individuals and

institutions around them. This over time creates "social guilt" and can be targeted by charitable causes. When a known person of wealth has hoarded funds, charity or faith-based projects must ask for gifts out of that bounty. "Ask not and receive not" is a firm truth in sacred scripture. In both sales and fundraising, one must "ask for the order." Do not hedge or be reluctant to ask for support for a worthy cause. Deep down people really do want to help. In fact wealthy folk are complimented when they are asked for donations. There is joy in giving because "It is more blessed to give that to receive." It should be remembered that if the wealthy are made to feel guilty because they do not support your projects, they may never give to that particular endeavor.

**Political Correctness**
Social guilt is akin to political correctness. The construct of correctness includes language, ideas, policies, and behavior seen as seeking to minimize social offense in certain contexts. It is alright to be nice to the wealthy, but do not patronize the rich; you will offend them. Be professional and balanced in an approach to people of means. Most individuals who gain wealth are knowledgeable of all the manipulative approaches in asking for money. One cannot tell a book by the cover nor can one evaluate the size of a gift from the wealthy. It is often based on "social guilt." When a person of means clearly understands the plight of the needy and compares the need to their available funds, a little social guilt may assist the individual in making a decision to support your cause. Even if you ask for more than the person could actually afford, you will not offend them. They are wealthy because they are wise and will simply say, "I can't give you $10,000 dollars today, but I could give you $2,000 today and about $4,000 next week. If you come back in about 90 days most likely I could have the other $4,000." It could be as easy as that to raise funds for a worthy cause. Never be afraid to ask.

**Social Equity**

Friendship is a wonderful thing. Friends are better than money in the bank because you can utilize the interest without depleting the principal. However, one should not presume that just because someone is a friend they will provide funds for your project or give to a cause. Be careful not to use social equity too often. Timing is important. Your friends may have a bad month just as others do and not have a cash flow to support your cause or to immediately comply with a request for funds. Pressing a friend to provide "cash now" can use up social equity quickly and this kind of equity is hard to rebuild. If your friends seem to avoid you, they probably think you will ask for money. Create opportunities for your friends to chat with you about your various projects. If they have available funds, they will share. Do not press the issue. Don't waste your social equity. Friends may be similar to a Certificate of Deposit at a bank: the funds are not immediately available without penalty. Remember CD's have a time lock and cashing in early causes a loss.

**Tithing of Time and Talent**

In addition to cash money, nonprofit enterprises need volunteers. Remember one can trade energy for cash and trade cash for labor. If one has funds, a person could be hired to do the work. Should one need funds they can actually apply to work. So cash and energy are two sides of the same coin. To increase volunteers for a nonprofit endeavor, encourage people to tithe their time or tithe their talent. They may not have cash but could work for you for four hours each week. Another may not have cash or the time to work for hours at a time, but they have talent as a musician and could give a benefit concert or come for one hour and play during dinner when you have possible donor guests. You see, there are several ways to bring in donations, and it doesn't even hurt.

**Sanctified Common sense**
The faith-based principles mentioned in this book are sanctified common sense and were formulated from lessons learned throughout life. Some of the "sanctified" lessons that became faith-based principles were used to develop the vision, mission, and projects such as the Bridge of Hope, the Anapausis community and other faith-based projects. I believe these principles are reproducible and could be used by others to continue similar development and programs. Some of these are listed in the appendix of this book.

**Perilous Times**
During troubled times people usually are willing to lay aside differences and join the effort to conquer the cause. These are perilous times and a small group of people have been chosen and some corporations have agreed to work with them to attack the poverty issues. The less fortunate and the poor cannot help themselves out of poverty. However, the Nation has sufficient wealth, available energy and programs to make a difference, **provided the concern can be turned into care and the care becomes commitment that leads to concerted activity in structured programs.** The poor do not need a hand-out; they need and want a hand up. Normally if someone will give the poor a hand, they will stand tall and become a productive citizen. Although some are "just takers," the chance to help some is worth the effort.

Just as any conflict or battle with opposition forces, it may not be possible to win the battle against poverty immediately and some remedial and surrogate work will be required to assist the disadvantaged children and dysfunctional families. If we can win their heart and soul, they will work with us in a long-term project. Gradually they will lift themselves out of a poor quality life and begin to strive for better circumstances for their family.

**Give hungry people food and they will be back tomorrow for more. Teach them how to grow a garden and they can**

**eventually feed themselves and their families.** If they are willing to plant a garden or take a job, assist them only until the first paycheck or the garden grows. Should they be unwilling to make the effort, provide your assistance where it will be appreciated. People who will not help themselves will never be prepared for a productive life. In other words, **all charity must be done with care and due diligence to be certain that those being helped are worthy of the assistance.**

**War against Poverty**
The war against poverty cannot be properly waged with a few; the masses must get involved. It is essential that such groups as the Anapausis Partnership and the Bridge of Hope make constructive efforts and launch workable projects to transform poverty into productivity and assist the poor to move beyond dependency. Once the poor have moved beyond depending on others for sustenance, care must be taken that those who have been assisted over the wall out of abject poverty do not develop an attitude of entitlement. Once outside forces have equipped the poor and their disadvantaged children with the tools and the resources to lift themselves out of poverty into a productive life, they must become self-sufficient and assume responsibility for their children and family. The goal would be that each family becomes self-supporting and that this is part of the answer to poverty.

**We put faith and investments in people and property because both appreciate in value over time.** As people grow, mature, and learn, their value increases just as when property is developed, the value is enhanced. Putting faith and trust in people assists their growth and development in many areas. When one feels trusted, work becomes easier. As one realizes that others have placed confidence and faith in them, they become more responsible and accountable both to themselves and to those who trusted and believed in them. This is especially true with children and young people.

In addition to sharing funds and resources, the most valued contribution to any worthy cause is actually labor. Every enterprise requires endless hours of physical, technical, and mental effort. When you provide yourself as a volunteer to assist a worthy cause, the project has a double blessing: 1) funds are conserved by not having to pay for the labor, and 2) the ministry of presence becomes an inspiration to others as well as assistance to the cause.

## Profitable Volunteerism

The secret to profitable volunteerism is the ability to listen and learn rather than attempting to tell others how to accomplish the task. God gave humans one mouth and two ears; therefore, it is concluded that listening is twice as important as talking. A volunteer must adopt the attitude that every person working in an organization or project can be a source of information. Listening to others then becomes the way to learn best how to do your part without interfering with others or the general plans of the endeavor. Volunteers should volunteer to listen and follow the guidance of those who have experience within the organization or program. Someone has to lead and others must follow.

## Networking is Important to our Mission

Networking with partners and building relationships is necessary to deliver goods and services. To do this: (1) identify and describe the partners assisting with various endeavors, (2) identify the Government offices that cooperate and work with Anapausis and Bridge of Hope, (3) identify and describe the organizations and groups that contribute to various aspects of the Anapausis vision, and (4) discover individual donors who will contribute to any of the enterprises or efforts advanced by the Anapausis vision.

## Social and Business Networking

When some people think of network, they assume it is social- izing with men and women in fancy suits, polite conversation and the exchanging of business cards; but I see social and business networking as a spiritual process of sharing a vision and a cause with people who are concerned about a common cause and have a sense of compassion for the less fortunate in society. I see networking as an interesting experience with people who are socially responsible and accountable to themselves for the support of a worthy cause. I see the process of working together with others for the common good as teamwork and partnering with God in caring for the needs of others.

**Focused and Guided**
Networking must be focused and guided by a sincere motive. The objective is not to take advantage of anyone but rather to provide others an opportunity to join the cause, share in the mission, and develop support for a worthy project. Making a connection with other individuals who may share your vision for a particular cause and perhaps will share in supporting a cause is an exciting adventure.

**My Understanding of Networking**
1. Networking is taking advantage of each opportunity to associate with others who may share my vision and who may be interested in and support projects or programs that advance the general mission.

2. Networking is being approachable and being friendly with those who may be interested in supporting the cause I want to advance.

3. Networking is about ideas, values, and interests. Gathering individuals who share a common desire to advance a particular mission or cause. It is about shared passion and shared opportunities to participate in a worthy cause or project.

4. Networking means spending a significant amount of time

engaging people and sharing with them my passion for a particular cause.

5. Networking is best accomplished in meeting people face-to-face. The Internet or other electronic technology may be used to establish initial contact, but networking requires personal contact. People want to see my personal passion and I want them to listen with the ear of their <u>**HEART**</u>. This often does not come through in alternative means of communication. Personal, face-to-face contact is the key to networking.

6. Networking is establishing and maintaining a relationship with others who share a common vision. When others see the concern and passion we share, they will catch the vision and assist the mission. A vision is more caught than taught.

7. Networking is teamwork and partnering with others to pass on information and to share in advancing a common cause for the common good.

**Networking Required**

Bridge of Hope recognizes Honored Partners through transparency of operation, available audits and engaging them in seminars and workshops. All sponsors are privy to advance plans and progress reports on projects they support.

**RECOGNITION PLAQUES
ARE DISPLAYED FOR HONORED PARTNERSHIP
AND MAJOR CONTRIBUTIONS:**

**The Australian Government contributed seed money for the Image Skills Centre at the Bridge of Hope.**

**The Guardian Holdings, Ltd. and Southern Sales & Service Company, Ltd. donated a mini-bus to Bridge of Hope.**

The Foundation for the Enhancement and Enrichment of Life (FEEL) and the umbrella organization known as Children's Villages Association of Trinidad and Tobago contributed to the Bridge of Hope concept.

Republic Bank Limited made possible the Bridge of Hope Business Centre.

Petroleum Women's Club contributed for pre-school and annual support.

Funds to construct a Dormitory:
Mr. & Mrs. Allan & Shella Saunders in memory of her mother, Amina Wajidali (Ma Ravello)

Funds to construct a Dormitory:
The family of Mr. Franklyn Capil-Nath, in his memory

Funds to construct an Orientation Facility
Mr. & Mrs. Tyrone Ramtahalsingh

United Way of Trinidad and Tobago
Annual Support

RBTT contributed to the
Educational Assessment Program

**Many Participants**
We acknowledge and appreciate the many participants who have contributed both funds and energy to various endeavors. There is not sufficient space to name them all, but our hearts and minds are filled with the memories of special assistance that met emergency needs and encouraged us on our journey.

Know that you are remembered in our daily prayers. Many of those who have assisted the Anapausis Partnership and demonstrated continued interest may participate in various ways in the Anapausis Society to perpetuate the vision and legacy. (See Chapter Ten.)

THE LOVE GATE

# CHAPTER NINE

## *GROWING NATION WITH GROWING NEEDS*

"The state of a nation is not judged by the infrastructure and buildings but by the prevalent attitude toward infants, children, families and the less fortunate."

Ω

"Without developing the children into moral and honorable citizens, there will be no viable state."

Ω

"The future of children in Trinidad and Tobago is in our hands."

Ω

"Look beyond the challenges of broken lives to the potential for a better life."

Ω

"No one including the poor and needy cares how much you know until you can convince them of how much you care."

Ω

"God's work done God's way never lacks God's supply."

Ω

"Normally we do not use the word "success" because it suggests more than enough; one can never do more than is needed."

**Prerequisite for a Moral Society**

It has been said that the state of a nation is not judged by the infrastructure and buildings but the prevalent attitude toward infants, children, families and the less fortunate. Roads, transportation, communication, commerce and trade and a functioning government are important for the present, but care for the children is crucial for the viability and sustainability of the culture and the nation. The infrastructure is needed, but the education and care of the children are indispensable. This is a prerequisite for a moral society and a wholesome environment to nurture a family. Without developing the children into moral and honorable citizens, there can be no viable state.

**A Macroeconomic Framework and Stability**
Trinidad and Tobago has a sound macroeconomic framework and a long tradition of institutional stability. The economy is primarily industrial, with an emphasis on petroleum and petrochemicals. It scores relatively well in most of the 10 economic freedoms, and its economy has grown at an average rate of close to 7 percent over the past five years. The government has tried to diversify the economic base, and the country has evolved into a key financial center in the Caribbean region. This means that the financial resources are available to the government to solve the abandonment problem that contributes to crime and family dysfunction. The wealth is available but there seems to be a lack of will to make the necessary reforms and enforce the existing laws to assure a safe and healthy place to live, work, and raise a family. In the midst of relative prosperity, crime has become a major problem.

Aristotle said many years ago, **"All who have meditated on the art of governing mankind have been convinced that the fate of empires depends on the education of youth."** The development of moral children in society could facilitate the resolution to many social problems. If children were brought up to know right from wrong, with a standard of conduct and moral behavior, then the incidence of social problems could be greatly reduced. Growing up with the knowledge of a Higher Power allows children to understand life, themselves, the society in which they exist, and their life purpose. The Psalmist wrote, "Thy word is a lamp unto my feet, and light unto my path" (119:105). And in the words of Gandhi, "You must be the change you wish to see in the world."

**Many Reasons for Abandonment**
Never were there so many reasons catalogued for neglected, abused, and abandoned children in Trinidad and Tobago and so little concern to fix the antecedent causes or to effect a workable intervention.   Some of the reasons have been identified, codified, and arranged into an organized presentation, but no solutions were presented.   Once the reasons for abandonment are known to exist and it is evident that these historical antecedents have led to abandonment for decades, why is there not a national outrage and intervention effort to break the cycle and give hope a chance to grow and guide the young to a productive life?   **It is a known fact that those who were abused continue to abuse others.**   Who will break this vicious cycle? The Anapausis Partnership is determined to do what is within the scope of reason and available resources to intervene in the areas that mostly affect children.

**Primary Causes of Abandonment**
Data from Viva Network Online shows the lack of education, poor housing, inadequate health care, child abuse, street children, prostitution and sexual exploitation are areas of concern where a small effort can make a big difference. The first three are primary issues of a responsible government. Past and present governments have programs in these areas, but the general public still seems to be indifferent to these issues.   Hopefully, future elected leaders will not only bring the resources of the national treasury to bear on these issues,

but will find a way to challenge the public to get involved in solving these national tragedies.

The other three areas identified above are more directly related to morality, human behavior, character, and family values. Although there are laws against child abuse, prostitution and sexual exploitation, these laws are not enforced sufficiently to make a difference. In fact some seem to take pleasure in the debased behavior of others and support it through music, events, movies, concerts, and other activities where alcohol, drugs, and sexual exploitation are apparent. What kind of message does this send to the youth of the present and children of the next generation? Hopefully, charity groups, faith-based entities, religious leaders, educators, stakeholders in corporations, and individual citizens will see the issue of child neglect, abuse, and abandonment and take personal action where it happens in their family and their community.

With anticipation and patience the vision and mission of the Anapausis Partnership includes working to solve the needs of children, whether it be housing, childcare, health, or education in the poorest villages of the country. Perhaps others will catch the vision and join in the effort to break the cycle of poverty and abuse. Possibly the policy makers of the nation will take notice of what a few are doing to alleviate the family and community problems and bring more governmental resources to support worthy projects.

It is my firm belief that the legal age at which children are able to do certain things adds to their risk. For example the legal age of sexual consent is 16 but The Marriage Act permits females to marry at age 12 and males at age 14. Marriage is permitted four years before a female is legally able to give sexual consent. Certain religions in Trinidad and Tobago have much higher standards for marriage, but some still permit marriage before the legal age of consent for females.

Children are at risk in Trinidad and Tobago and what is being done is too little, too late. More must be done by government, NGO's, faith-based organizations, private citizens, and parents to protect and care for disadvantaged children. Somehow the cycle of abandonment, abuse, and neglect must be stopped. The exploitation of children is against the law. Officials must enforce the child protection laws and encourage parents and communities to do their part. Custodial care facilities can only provide a safety-net for a few. Perhaps the government could require more FamilyLife instructions at the time of marriage or when family members are brought to court for abuse or neglect.

Crime is as old as Trinidad and Tobago itself, going back to the 17th and 18th centuries when the islands were a haven for pirates. Recently, crime has become a major topic of discussion among the citizens. Whether there is a serious crime situation or merely the media exaggerating and exploiting what does happen, the perception is that criminal activity has been and still is a controversial topic on the two islands. Murders have risen every year since 1999. About 500 people are murdered annually on our twin islands.

**An Area of Concern**
Education is a general area of concern for the citizens. Data from the Ministry of Education (National Policy on Student Support Services) shows that 75 percent of the children are intellectually below normal or have difficulties related to sensory problems. Only two percent demonstrate in the gifted category. This shows the scope of the problems just in education alone. Since the lack of education was one of the antecedent causes of abandonment, educational

improvements are desperately needed to assist with relieving the problem of abandoned children. Quality expansion is needed in the area of education. The Bridge of Hope mission and the Anapausis vision includes several aspects of education.

## 'Children at Risk' in Trinidad and Tobago

Data from Viva Network Online lists 48 areas where children are at risk:

1. **abandonment**
2. **abortion**
3. **adolescent motherhood**
4. **bereavement**
5. **child abuse**
6. **child disappearance**
7. **child-headed households**
8. **child labour**
9. **child trafficking**
10. **criminal activity**
11. **cultural influence**
12. **disability**
13. **disease**
14. **divorce**
15. **drought and natural disasters**
16. **economic problems/national debt**
17. **family disintegration**
18. **forced marriage**

19. gender specific risk
20. HIV/AIDS
21. inadequate health care
22. inadequate sanitation
23. infant mortality
24. injury
25. imprisonment
26. injustice
27. internet
28. lack of contraception
29. lack of education
30. loss of parents/orphanhood
31. low birth weight
32. mental disability
33. political problems
34. poor housing
35. poor maternal health
36. poor nutrition/malnutrition
37. post traumatic stress disorder
38. poverty
39. prostitution and sexual exploitation
40. psychological trauma
41. racial prejudice
42. refugees and displacement
43. rural-urban migration
44. single parent families
45. street children
46. subsance abuse

**47. unemployment**

**48. urbanization**

## Additional Research

In addition to others who are researching the problems and trends of Trinidad and Tobago, those connected with the Anapausis Vision are searching, surveying, and discovering growing needs in the nation. As needs are assessed and as funds are available, projects and programs are put in place to service the need to the best of our ability with the resources and the people available.

As the nation grows so do the needs of the children multiply. Since the basic family and community problems have not been solved, the number of needy children continues to grow. With this growing need there must be new and innovative efforts to save the children, restore families, improve communities, and make the nation what the founders desired.

THE LOVE GATE

# CHAPTER TEN

## *CAMPAIGN TO BUILD CHAMPIONS*

"Look beyond the challenges of broken lives to the
potential for a better life."

Ω

"No one including the poor and needy cares how much you
know until you can convince them of how much you care."

Ω

"God is a God of 'another chance' not just a second chance."

Ω

"Your influence is positive when you are a good example in
all aspects of life."

Ω

"Lead by example in every aspect of both personal and
professional life."

Ω

"Grow and blossom where you are planted."

"Never look at a half-full glass; see it filled, half with something
and half with air.  Then come to the knowledge that God is
spirit and fills the whole world and that the balance of a half-
full glass is filled with the spirit and presence of God."
Ω
"Live a life larger than yourself and work together with God in
the areas of the greatest need."
Ω
"God put us together not only to help each other, but to work
together for the good of others.
Ω
"One should tithe both time and talent."
Ω

## Faith-based Principles Make a Difference
Starting with the Ten Commandments from the Torah and
appearing in various forms in other religions to the Golden
Rule in the New Testament, we are stewards of both the
instructions and the resources God provides.  The Golden
Rule is so basic it appears in most of the religions of the
world. For example:

- **Buddhism** –"Hurt not others in ways that you yourself would
  find hurtful" (Udana-Vaarga 5,1)
- **Christianity** –"As you would that men should do unto you, do
  you also to them likewise." (Luke 6:31)
- **Hinduism** – "This is the sum of duty; do naught unto others
  what you would not have them do unto you."
  (Mahabharata 5, 1517)
- **Judaism** – "What is hateful to you, do not do to your fellowman.
  This is the entire Law; all the rest is commentary." (Talmud,
  Shabbat 3id)
- **Taoism** – "Regard your neighbor's gain as your gain, and your
  neighbor's loss as your own loss." (Tai Shang Kan Yin P'ien)

## An Incredible Time
The young years are an incredible time of learning and growth,
and we want to make sure that all the children at Bridge of Hope

learn spiritual truths, develop educationally, and maintain a healthy life-style. We want them to become champions and be productive members of society. While they are in the care of the home, these things can be supervised and controlled. The difficulty is what happens to them after they come of age and leave Bridge of Hope for the real world. We are aware that the home presents an insulated environment, a kind of cocoon they must exit into the work-a-day world.

**Bridging the Gulf**
As each young person leaves the home we are assured that they are better off than had they continued in their previous environment; however, family ties are strong and one fear is that they may reconnect with the negative aspects of the previous arrangements. This is why we must develop an aftermarket, a post-custodial care plan to bridge the fixed gulf between custodial care and the real world of work. We want to call this plan Campaign to Build Champions.

**Thinking Positively**
Henry Ford coined the phrase: **"If you think you can, or think you can't - you're right!"** This means that by thinking positively, the brain will create the circumstances that produce achievement. The concept is simple. By maintaining a positive attitude, young people will dress the part, look the part, say the right thing at the right time, and generally be attractive to the people around them. No one wants to be around negative people. Positive thinking is a basic ingredient of progress.

**Keys to the Model of Philanthropy**
Mentoring and coaching were keys to developing a model of philanthropy. A goal of all my social, business, and spiritual endeavors was to create a reproducible model of support, benefaction, investment, sponsorship, accountability, and direct and indirect aid to the needy. My desire was to express generosity in a socially responsible way and to raise

benevolence to a more spiritual level that created a higher awareness of human needs.  Helping others was both direct and indirect in a manner that was soft and sincere to improve the general welfare of those in need.  To do this required a great deal of mentoring of individuals in the form of advising, counseling, guiding, teaching by example, and direct tutoring. This was done to reproduce common-sense lessons and translate them into faith-based principles that could change the attitudes and practices of others.

The developing model included a great deal of team-type and personal coaching that incorporated hands-on experience and personal guidance as to how some things could be done differently; how other things could be done better, and how new things could be done that would solve personal, family and community problems and improve the quality of life for those involved. A model is of little value unless it is understood and reproduced.  It is suggested that the reader review the common-sense lessons and the faith-based principles and, after careful consideration, take the nectar from those that are personally meaningful and make their own honey...look at your own life-lessons, develop your own principles and model of philanthropy.

**Brains and Pains**
One young man who thought he was not bright said, **"When they passed out brains, I thought they said 'pains' so I hid behind the door."** He had not learned that "taking pains to do something" was similar to "having the brains to do something." The concept of "pains" not only describes many of the hurts that come to the disadvantaged, but the word also suggests "care, effort, thoroughness, and attention to detail" necessary to make progress or accomplish something. In organized athletics coaches often tell the players there is "no gain without pain."  This means that growth and progress come with great personal effort and usually some discomfort.

**Growing Pains**
It is normal to experience "growing pains" as a part of the maturing process and progress in life. Some think they can simply practice the same old stuff day after day and that persistence alone will produce progress or success. This is a tragic fault of many who fail in their endeavors. There must be consistent effort, but also planning and the use of common sense is required. Keeping a journal of activities can assist in producing variety into a project and assist in understanding areas of weakness that hinder progress. This means change. One must develop an entrepreneurial spirit, become creative and take the risk. Caution! All ventures into new areas carry an element of risk. There are hazards in most undertaking. A wrong move could cause a human setback in the process of assisting others. This is why one must take "pains" to do it right. Starting over is a hard thing to do. There is an old saying, **"Why is there never enough time to do it right, but always sufficient time to do it over?"**

**Producing Champions requires Mentoring and Coaching**
When your overall philosophy is to invest your life in service to others, you will empower the needy and build them into champions. Invest in the young and grow winners. This can be done in five (5) steps: (1) **Caring** for the very young; (2) **Educating** the children; (3) **Training** the youth; (4) **Preparing** young people for life and work, and (5) **Producing** moral and productive citizens to become champions in the real world.

**Growing Champion Roses**
Building champions is similar to growing roses. Roses can sometimes be finicky and difficult to grow, and they definitely require care. One cannot just plant a rose bush and forget about it and expect it to grow into a champion rose. However, if one picks the correct rose for the climate and plants it with care, growing a champion rose is something that the average citizen could do. The rose-growing community provides an

easy step-by-step instruction plan.  A similar plan is usable to the building of champions.

## Application to Building Champions

Once a young man or woman leaves the private "lighthouse" known as custodial care, they find themselves in the cold and unfriendly world of reality.   Just as the rose that buds and blooms, they will be moved to a more public place for all to see. Perhaps this strategy for growing champion roses could be adapted for the Campaign to Build Champions.

**1.      Choose** the right rose from your garden and pick an area to plant to receive the morning sun and at least six hours of sunshine daily.

**Application:** Select from among those exiting custodial care those who need additional care.  House them where the sunlight can overcome the darkness and they can receive continued guidance and care to adapt to the new environment.

**2.      Soak** the roots of the rose plant in water several minutes before planting.

**Application:**  Saturate the roots of the young person with special care and attention in the final days before they leave custodial care.  Make them feel a sense of belonging and that they are not alone. Remind them of what they have learned and the opportunity for a better life they were provided.

**3.      Cut** off any dead or damaged ends on the roots.

**Application:** Correct any final behavior problems and deal with all possible liabilities that could hinder their adjustment to the real world.  Call attention to the areas where they have needed correction and remind them that these old habits become dead weight and will cut down their opportunities in the real world.

**4.** **Dig** a hole for the rose plant that is at least two times the size of the root system. Put organic matter into the hole when planting. Mulch the surface of the garden to provide nutrients and hinder the growth of weeds and prevent the soil from drying too quickly.

**Application:** Make a place for the young person to grow. They need space but also some special mulch to provide food and some care and attention to keep the weeds from growing and choking out the potential future and opportunity.

**5.** **Water** the roots not the foliage to prevent fungal disease. Water the roots daily for the first few weeks after planting in order to grow champion roses. After the first month give the garden a good deep soaking every couple of weeks.

**Application:** Follow-up daily for the first few weeks then plan monthly visits to maintain a connection and provide opportunities for interaction with a friend.

**6.** **Fertilize** the rose according to the directions on the rose food, but stop before the major dry spell.

**Application:** Read the directions on each young person and provide the required elements for healthy growth and development.

**7.** **Prune** the rose bush in early spring. Start by removing any dead or damaged branches. Permit only the five or six healthiest branches to remain.

**Application:** Make adjustments to behavior and environment by removing all items and individuals that would damage the future of the young person. The easy and convenient thing may work today, but building better character and providing excellent tools will break the old and bad habits and lead to a self-sufficient lifestyle.

**A Four-Step Plan**
Common-sense Lessons that become faith-based principles for living should be used to build the character of young men and women in order to strengthen their moral fiber and build them into champions. When one commits 100% to the goal and knows what the target dates and deadlines are a workable game plan can be created.

Let them become creative. Teach them how to network. Coach them in selling themselves and their talents to potential employers. Help them stay positive and develop a "can do" attitude. Guide them in writing a personal plan for the next six months of their life. What are their goals? Who will be their friends and associates? How will they earn a living? How will they manage their money? Once their plan is in place they will grow in confidence. Then the maturing process will take hold and they will grow into productive citizens.

**Four-Step Plan:**
**Know—Share—Watch—See.**

**1.      Know the individual:** The more one knows about the young person leaving custodial care and moving into the adult arena, the more assistance one can provide. Each person is different and one size does not fit all. The plans may be similar, but they must be tailored to the individual. Living space, job opportunities, free time activities, and regular contacts with true friends.

**2.      Share a plan for the future:** It is a fearful thing to leave home and step into the unknown without a friend and plan. Lay everything out in writing. Use the K.I.S.S. formula: "Keep it Simple and Short. Go over the plan several times with the individual before they leave custodial care. Make them feel the plan is tailored just for them and that they must follow it or ask for permission to make changes. They must never feel they are totally on their own. For at least six months they must be monitored, counseled, and encouraged.

**3.      Watch them grow:**   The most wonderful part of this difficult task is to watch a young person mature and grow. Let them make a few mistakes, everyone does. Simply call their attention to the unacceptable behavior with tough love. There must be consequences to straying from the plan. If they refuse to work with you, then give them a warning that in two weeks they will be totally on their own. This means they pay the rent, buy the food, provide transportation, manage their money, and live the best they can. Be nice, but firm!

**4.      See them serve:**   Those who follow the agenda prepared for them and mature and grow may need guidance as to how they can give back to those who assisted them over the troubled waters of the past and brought them into the land of opportunity. Teach them to serve and develop a volunteer spirit. In other words encourage them to find ways and means to assist others. All champions play fair, work with the team, and share the glory of victory. Occasionally help them celebrate!

**Transition from Custodial Care to the Real World**
The Bridge of Hope needs assistance from partners to develop the transition plan for children coming out of custodial care in Trinidad and Tobago and moving into the real world. Unless this is accomplished soon much of the good that custodial facilities have accomplished could be lost.

The transition from custodial care to the real world is a shock to the whole human system. Young people who grow up with a two-parent and stable home life often have problems when the go off to college, get a job in the next town, or marry and start their own family. Children who have negative images of their real family and have been isolated in custodial care need special transitional training and guidance several months before they leave custodial care. Also, they need a safe place to live and work in the first few months or even years after leaving the direct control and influence of caregivers. This must become a priority.

**Transitional Training**
Several months before leaving custodial care young men and women who have been under close supervision for years need special training. Some six to nine months prior to release a concerted effort should be made to prepare them for the real world. The training curriculum should include:

- Money Management
- Housekeeping and Home Economics
- Buying Groceries and Meal Preparation
- Basic Recipes and Cooking Instructions
- Sharing Household Chores
- Dealing with a House Mate
- Choosing Friends and Associates
- Dating Guidelines
- Daily Devotions and Church Attendance
- Basic Household Maintenance
- Use of Local Transportation System
- Completing Job Application
- Job Interviewing
- Email and Cell Phone Etiquette
- Listening Techniques
- Further Education Guidance
- Guidelines for Good Study Habits
- Guidelines for Seeking Counsel or Getting Answers

- Basic First Aid and Medical Contacts
- Self-concept and Self-image
- Communication and Listening Skills

**How to Behave toward Staff and Management of the Home who cared for them during their time of need.**
Teach them how to be a good alumnus of the home and be proud of it. Guidelines on how to give back would be appropriate.

# PLANNED EXPANSION
## Guided by a Vision

### Research by Canadians
Canadian visitors surveyed the area around Bridge of Hope and discovered many young women with children under school age. This pointed out the need for a Day Care Nursery for these children so the mother, being a single parent, could get out of the home and find employment. As a result of this research, a Day Care Nursery Unit is planned as a kind of "mother's nursery."

Providing the space at Bridge of Hope for a Day Care Nursery would not be difficult with a sponsor for funding; however, the primary difficulty is the mature caregiver required to care for such needy children. To be sufficiently accommodating for the number of pre-school-aged children needing day care would require at least three additional staff at Bridge of Hope unless the planned Senior Homes could be built in a timely manner in proximity to the campus. Also, additional equipment would be required in terms of infant furniture for sleeping and play. There would be a need for special food for the undernourished. Bridge of Hope seeks sponsors for the addition to their care and community service. This sponsorship would do three things: 1) enhance the program of Bridge of Hope, 2) provide needed care for the youngest and most at risk children in the community, and 3) free the single mother to seek employment to better care for herself and her child.

## The Challenge of Transition

A major challenge for Bridge of Hope is the transition from custodial care to the real world. When children have lived in the confines of custodial care for several years, they cannot be turned out to care for themselves in the harsh world without a period of special training and supervision. We can teach and train them in money management, housekeeping skills, finding employment, sharing the chores of living, buying food and cooking meals, but more is needed. Young people coming out of custodial care need a safe place to mentally, physically, socially, and spiritually make the transition to the real world. The growing vision includes future transition housing projects for young men and women coming out of several custodial care facilities in Trinidad and Tobago to serve the transitional needs and bridge the gap from custodial care to the real world. These will be called Home Unit Groups (HUG) Homes and will be clustered in a compound facility with security and supervision. This will assist the vision that includes a perpetual campaign to build champions to be high achievers and become productive citizens of Trinidad and Tobago.

## Surrogate Grandparents Needed

There is also a growing need for the children in custodial care to have surrogate grandparents to supply some of the missing elements in a child's life. Debbie and I have learned valuable lessons from our grandparents, and we believe it would be helpful for the children in places such as Bridge of Hope to have a connection with older, mature, and wiser individuals. Staff in the custodial care facilities do a good job, but their time is limited and with so many children with individual needs, more volunteer assistance is needed. We hope to construct a series of senior homes in connection with Bridge of Hope and screen the occupants to provide quality surrogate "grandparents" for the children. This would fill a void in the life of the children.

## Senior Citizens Housing Units

The volunteer work of Kenrick Frost, Debbie's father, at Bridge of Hope has made us aware of the serious need for the presence of seniors at the home. This is why we proposed Olive's House in proximity to Bridge of Hope. The children need surrogate grandparents and the elderly need to be needed and want to share their knowledge with children. Mrs. Olive Frost, Debbie's paternal grandmother left "seed money" to initiate the project. There is space at the back of the Bridge of Hope to build this unit. An Architect will produce plans. When plans are approved and funds are available, construction will begin. We seek sponsors to fund the construction of the individual family units in Olive's House. The compound will be known as Olive's House, but the individual units may be named for donors. We seek funds for "naming gifts."

Olive's House would be a guest house approach to condo-type units in a single building to better utilize space and material. The unit would have a common area or gathering place for special meals, mail, laundry, fellowship and places to entertain family and friends. The vision is to construct Olive's House near the Bridge of Hope compound and secure seniors with moral character who have lived an honorable life to occupy each unit. They would pay a small stipend out of their pension income and be able to treat the unit as a home. Living in proximity to the children, Bridge of Hope personnel would conduct a Skills Survey to determine what each senior could and would be willing to do in relation to the children and the home. Some could teach gardening, others could teach home economics. Still others could work with the staff depending on their qualifications. The plan is to permit their talent and skills to make a place for them to serve the children and the Bridge of Hope.

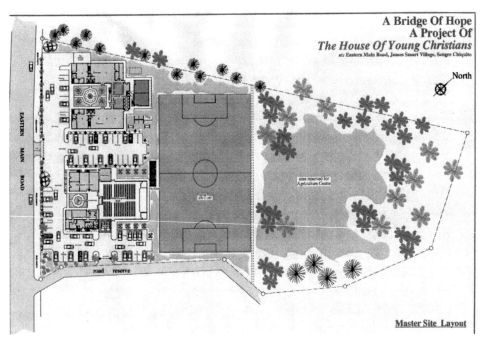

A Bridge Of Hope
A Project Of
*The House Of Young Christians*
at: Eastern Main Road, James Smart Village, Sangre Chiquito

North

area reserved for Agriculture Centre

road    reserve

Master Site Layout

**The Olive's House for seniors and surrogate grandparents of the children will be constructed when plans are approved by the Directors and funds are available. The space to the right of the present complex is proposed. Olive's House will also house some support staff for the Bridge of Hope.**

Serving as surrogate grandparents, teachers, coaches, life-guides, or tutors for growing children would be an exciting way to spend the declining years of life. This project would add value and meaning to the lives of the elderly and leverage their skills and competence to create a productive enterprise for mutual benefits. Children always bring joy to the heart and soul of the elderly. There is a need for senior homes in proximity to Bridge of Hope to supply these surrogate grandparents for the children and to give the elderly a useful life and a way to pass on the lessons they learned during their long life. This is vital to the full development of children. They need the mature influence of senior adults who have lived a moral and productive life. Normally, if an adult is asked to remember those who had the most influence on their life they recall grandparents, old uncles or aunts, older brothers or sisters, older teachers and seniors in the community. We must provide this element for their full development before they leave custodial care to become productive citizens. This will better prepare them for aftercare as they move to the HUG Homes

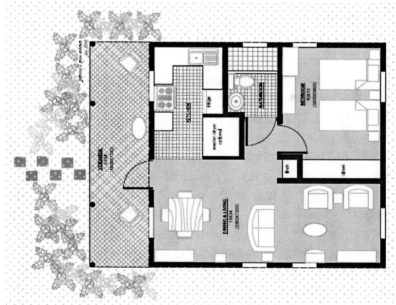

**A preliminary plan for a senior unit in Olive's House was suggested by Architect Patricia Elaine Green.**
**Other unit plans will be considered.**

## Home Unit Group (HUG) Homes

It has been said that an individual needs seven (7) hugs each day of their life. In a busy world many people are short on wholesome hugs. Hopefully, those young people coming out of custodial care will find not just a token hug when they leave the facility, but some kind of secure place to call home for the months of transition. We propose a set of group homes for this purpose. Perhaps it could be called **Home Unit Group (HUG) Housing.** If not an actual facility then those coming out of custodial care could be grouped and placed in **HUG** living quarters. These compatible groups could assist in the transition.

The planned construction would be a compound-type complex with several two-story units that house four young people (two downstairs and two upstairs) coming out of custodial care. The HUG Homes would be placed in a dual cluster environment with one section for young men and one section for young women. Access to the upper level would be outside the units to protect the privacy of each group. A central two-story unit for adult supervision would be placed in the center of the compound separating the young men and women in the HUG Homes. The upstairs would house a supervising couple and a common gathering place downstairs would be used for occasional meals, mail, laundry, fellowship and entertaining friends. The vision is for a group of cluster homes to house four young men or four young women coming out of custodial care.

These young people would be required to take a six months transition course before leaving custodial care, sign a behavior and work contract, pay rent and general care for their own needs. Sponsors would be assigned to interact with them and to be on call if they are needed. These homes would be used as transition facilities and would be temporary housing for individuals exiting custodial care. These homes would be more than a half-way house. We want to make a good and full transition to productive life for the young people for whom we have invested so much time and energy.

We envision homes that house four (4) compatible individuals leaving custodial care. To qualify for HUG housing the young people would have to be processed through a structured exiting course that deals with all aspects of leaving the custodial structure for the less structured real world such as paying rent and utilities, buying groceries and preparing meals, sharing and doing housekeeping chores, getting a job, and managing money. There would also be guidance as to how to choose friends and associates and the dating rules. How to maintain good relationships with other house-mates would be a primary effort.

Individuals would sign a one-year contract and make certain agreements with the parent custodial care facility to allow a certain degree of supervision and accountability. The young men and women would also be assigned guidance counselors or senior mentors who will work with them during the first year of transition. After the first year, provided there is agreement of both parties the individuals may sign an extension to include the second year. However, both the custodial care facility sponsors and the young person must agree that staying an extra year would be beneficial.

**HUG Home Guidance/Mentors Needed**
Once the HUG Homes are built for the transition of young people to the real world, we need couples to occupy the compound and provide supervision, mentoring and coaching for both young men and young women who do not have the guidance of parents or grandparents. *Contact Debbie or myself directly if you are interested in this ministry to young people.*

**#1 Anapausis, Upper Mohammed Street, Curepe,
Trinidad & Tobago
Home: (868) 663-3518; Mobile (868) 354-7319
Email: subdeb10@gmail.com**

**Sponsors, Donors, and Volunteers are Needed**
Bridge of Hope seeks sponsors for the addition to their care and community service. This sponsorship would do three things: (1) enhance the program of Bridge of Hope, (2) provide needed care for the youngest and most at risk children in the community, and (3) free the single mother to seek employment to better care for herself and her child. Not only do we seek support for the Day Care Nursery, we need assistance with the Senior Homes and the Home Unit Groups (HUG) housing for young men and women leaving custodial care. We need this assistance promptly and will arrange for naming gifts to construct and furnish the facilities. Potential donors and sponsors may contact Debbie or myself directly. Senior Couples interested in living on the Bridge of Hope campus in the Senior Home complex should contact us and get your names on the list.

**In the final analysis it is not what you do for the children, but what you have taught them to do for themselves that will make them successful human beings.**
**- – Ann Landers**

The purpose of the endeavors described in this book was to grow children into responsible adults. Admittedly, we were not always successful with each child that God placed in our care. It should be noted that Bridge of Hope received children at different ages and most already had negative influences ingrained into their behavior. We also worked with mature adults in an effort to create an awareness of the needs of children and to generate more aggressive programs and projects to assist the needy.

The best environment to grow champions is a stable two parent family living together in a caring atmosphere. Custodial care is not ideal; it is a remedial effort to make productive citizens from disadvantaged or abandoned children. Childcare workers assisting in the endeavors covered in this book were only human and not the actual parents of the children; therefore, they operated with limitations. Just as some children turn out differently than the hopes and dreams of parents, those responsible for guiding the footsteps of children at the Bridge of Hope home had different levels of achievement with each child. This usually depends on the age the child enters custodial care. Here are some positive testimonials in support of the concepts and endeavors presented in this book.

**Good Judge of Character**
A good way to judge the character of an adult is to ask young people with whom they have been associated. On several occasions a Canadian Youth Pastor, Dave Easton, and a group of young people from Canada came to Trinidad to work with the House of Young Christians and the Bridge of Hope. When these young workers were asked for their thoughts about Subesh and Debbie a wealth of replies were received. Here is a composite of some of the things young workers remember about working with the Ramjattans:

> My favorite quote from my times in Trinidad was on the wall of the old children's home just outside the kitchen; **"If you release what is in your hands for God, then He will release what is in His hands for you."** This echoed Subesh's statement, "Take care of God's business and God will take care of your business."

> Few people in the world have made a more substantial difference in the positive social development of a nation than this couple. They have shown real heart for the disadvantaged over many years of service to the abandoned and abused children of Trinidad. They have a passion for equipping and training people to enable them to move beyond their inherited poverty. Their work is the embodiment of the ideals that produce positive social change.

> Subesh and Debbie have looked beyond the challenges of broken lives to the potential for a better life. They seem to have a

special joy in serving the poor and even more so with assisting
abandoned and abused children. No one including the poor and
needy cares how much you know until you can convince them of
how much you care.

We always learned a lot about God on our visits to Trinidad. God
never wastes a hurt. God is a God of 'another chance' not just a
second chance. God blesses you to be a blessing to others. God
calls us to be faithful, not successful. Normally we do not use the
word "success" because it suggests more than enough; one can
never do more than is needed. God's work done God's way never
lacks God's supply.

Your influence is positive when you are a good example in all
aspects of life. Lead by example in every aspect of life, both
personal and professional. Grow and blossom where you are
planted. It is not go and do, but do as you go; in reality it is work
in your own environment, in your "Jerusalem." Look around you,
there are needy children in close proximity to you. It has been
said that a human being can live about forty days without food,
four days without water, and four minutes without air: but only a
miserable life without hope.

Every human being one meets regardless of their station in
life can add something worthwhile to ones knowledge and
experience. Never look at a half-full glass; see it filled, half with
something and half with air. Then come to the knowledge that
God is spirit and fills the whole world and that the balance of a
half-full glass is filled with the spirit and presence of God. Never
show inconsistency in dealing with disadvantaged children, they
have already witnessed sufficient discrepancy and contradiction
in their previous environment.

Always invest in people, property and poverty, all will increase in
value and the effort produces a good return on the investment of
time, energy, and funds.

## Other Testimonials

### Caring and Selfless People
The hope of a better life just vanished with the challenges of
each day until I became part of the Bridge of Hope family. Being

abandoned at the age of eight with two younger brothers; Kevin and Andy, life was hard and daily living difficult without parents or any real source of food. At Bridge of Hope I met Subesh and Debbie Ramjattan, two of the most caring and selfless people I know, two people who gave their lives to obey the call of God. They dedicated their time, effort and energy pouring into me their life experiences, their knowledge, and valuable nuggets so that I could become a responsible man willing to stand up and help others in need. They have treated me as one of their own sons, opening my eyes to see life from a different perspective. Because of them I have learned to grab each opportunity that came my way. I am forever grateful for the relationship that I share with these two people and for all the lessons learned from exposure to their lives. My exposure to the Bridge of Hope and the Anapausis Community has taught me that "When God has a plan for your life; no one or no circumstance can hold you back."
– **Rakesh Ramkissoon. Administrative Assistant at the House of Marketing Ltd.**

## An Example and Inspiration

I want to thank you for the encouraging role you have played in my life. Whether you realize it or not, God has used you as an example and inspiration to me. The way that you serve Him so faithfully and the commitment you have made to give so generously and serve so wholeheartedly has challenged me to do the same. As I step out in faith to serve God and to trust in His provision, I draw strength from those who have set such a great example. May God continue to bless both of you as you shepherd with integrity of heart and lead with skillful hands.... (Ps. 78:72).
– **Rhondi Fowler, Youth Pastor in Canada.**

## My Father Figure and Spiritual Mentor

Living with an abusive and drug addicted father, I was at a crossroads when Subesh Ramjattan came into my life as a father figure and a spiritual mentor. Always positive and encouraging, he taught me to be responsible, encouraged my further education and always included me in workshops and seminars to develop my full potential. He was never judgmental but always offered advice as a way of guiding me and building my self-esteem. His guidance assisted me in finding my life's purpose, helping me set goals and plan strategies to achieve those goals. He urged

me to "do the little things well and bigger things would follow."
He was always generous in sharing his wealth of knowledge and
experience, what he called "sharing my gray hairs."
My present accomplishments were possible because Mr.
Ramjattan encouraged my relationship with God. As a spiritual
leader, Subesh approached me with a spirit of humility and
service. It was this attitude that attracted me to him. He stressed
spiritual matters and led me to a profession of faith and baptism
in January 2006. God has truly blessed this man with a gift of
vision and determination to see things through. Subesh has been
effective in all his business and charity endeavors. His famous
saying "I don't want to know the storms you've encountered, just
bring the ship to shore" is truly indicative of his nature. If you
interact with Subesh Ramjattan, you will get to know one of the
most genuine, selfless human beings to ever walk this earth.
— **Riaz Ali, Bridge of Hope Administrator of Community Services**

## Someone Extraordinary

When I first met Subesh Ramjattan I knew immediately that I
had just met someone extraordinary. His passion combined with
his vision and his ability to turn that vision into reality makes
him incredibly unique. As the founder of Bridge of Hope and the
Kernahan Center, he has used his life experiences, his talents,
and his resources to change the lives of countless children at
risk and others in need. It is a rare individual who can take what
most people only dream about and turn it into a reality.

He is a man who cares deeply about his country and his
community. He is passionately committed to the children and
individuals that cross his path. For these children, he not only
meets their physical needs in an incredible way but more than
that he is passionate about their minds, their hearts and their
souls. He works with incredible energy and enthusiasm to
ensure that every child has the opportunity to succeed in life. By
creating true change in the lives of these children and, in turn,
his community and country as a whole, he leaves a legacy of an
improved future for many generations to come. He is a source
of inspiration to all those around him and I count it a true honor
and privilege to know this man of God.– **Beth Shanklin, Founder/
Executive Director Child Development International, Inc.**

## Evident Love and Compassion

I was fortunate that Subesh Ramjattan intervened in my life. While on child care staff at Bridge of Hope he inspired and encouraged me to chart a course that would lead me to a special place of service. As the head teacher in a village that was described as, "being behind God's back," in an under-developed area in Trinidad, I found my place to serve.

The evident love and compassion Subesh has for people, especially children who are in desperate situations, was an inspiration to me. I wanted to share his vision of bringing a better life to other children. By his encouragement and support, he has been a big influence in my life. He is an inspiration because he is a man of God, who doesn't only "Talk the Talk." He "Walks the Walk." – **Charmaine Jill Ramsingh, Head Teacher, Kernahan Early Childhood Care and Education Centre**

## A Supportive Employer and Friend

I met Subesh Ramjattan at a businessmen's meeting and approached him to inquire about employment at his company. The next day I visited his office and he offered me a job. Over the next 14 years Subesh was a supportive employer and friend and had a positive impact on my life. During my time at his company, I observed his style of business management and many other professional development ideas, which are now embedded in me. Over those years, Subesh and I have developed a great relationship of trust and respect for each other. He was, and still is, like a father to me. Our association has always remained cordial and professional.

Mr. Ramjattan has inspired me to pursue my own business ventures and, even though, I no longer work at the House of Marketing, he has retained my services on the boards of two of his subsidiary companies. I will always be grateful to Mr. Ramjattan since he helped me build my first home and set up insurance policies for my three children. He is a selfless, giving and caring person. He is loyal, honest and religious, and for these virtues I continue to admire him. — **Sterling Parris**

## No Stone Unturned for Social Justice

God orchestrated my path to Subesh Ramjattan. Subesh approached me about serving at Bridge of Hope; I was excited as he guided me into areas of service beyond my experience. He believed in my ability. When everyone else would give up, Subesh continues to have an abundance of grace and faith in a person's ability and willingness to realize their potential. He has an eye for special gifts in people and foresees a pathway for those gifts to materialize for the benefit of mankind. His desire to see people rise up and go beyond their ability comes from an overwhelming passion to see people excel.

Subesh has walked a path that pulls on the strings of my own heart. He is a proactive mentor who practices what he preaches and has encouraged me to always be prepared, controlling situations through preparation. He invests his extensive corporate and personal experiences to inspire and empower me to be the best for the future but takes the time to impart his wisdom to help me to grow now. His transferable coaching and mentoring skills have a built in process of duplication, because many have been successful just being around him. It gives truth to the expression that a vision "Is easier caught than taught."

Subesh has an unconditional love for humanity. Race, color or class make no difference. He leaves no stone unturned in helping people rise above challenging and life-threatening situations. These attributes make him a man of the heart, connecting with people everywhere he goes. Having a strong mentor giving guidance and coaching provides a sounding board for ideas, the chance to avoid common mistakes, and the opportunity to learn. Working and walking with him as my mentor helps me concentrate and refine my strengths to avoid common mistakes and reinforce my weaknesses. The legacy of Mr. Subesh Ramjattan will live and impact generations to come! I am blessed to glean from his life. – **Anne-Marie Morrison, Administrator of Bridge of Hope**

## A tribute to the Ramjattans

The Anapausis Community has become the venue for an annual FamilyLife conference which has touched numerous couples and healed many marriages. The Ramjattans desire FamilyLife and Education to be emphasized and they are happiest when

Anapausis is being used for those reasons. However, their passion goes deeper than Anapausis being a venue just for an occasional conference – they dream of seeing Anapausis touching families on an ongoing basis and this has been demonstrated by some monthly outreaches to include entire families. Their genuine care and concern have continued through the years.

Subesh and Debbie are transparent and are always seeking to help those in need. Subesh constantly brings persons to my office to assist me with networking. Both he and Debbie earnestly desire to be used in the expansion of the Lord's kingdom and this is shown in tangible ways, such as the Bridge of Hope and Kernahan projects, in addition to the Anapausis Community. They have a humility about them which is refreshing and sets them apart as special in today's society. It is my great joy to know and interact with them, and I wish to pay special tribute to them for the blessing they are to me and my work.
–Margaret Beekee, Campus Crusade for Christ, TT

## Making a Real Difference

It is now a decade since I met Subesh Ramjattan. He surprised me at the start. My wife and I had just come home from a holiday in Tobago and discovered that someone had broken into our apartment. We were so shaken by this violation of our personal space. Subesh heard about this difficulty and offered to relocate us the next day into a spare apartment in his Anapausis home. Imagine this stranger, understanding our need at the time, and reaching out to us in such a big way! We stayed nine months at Anapausis, and in that time, deepened our relationship with Subesh and Debbie. We also discovered that our experience was not unique. Subesh and Debbie were doing this for many other people and making a real difference in their lives.

After we left Anapausis, I started partnering with Subesh in various projects. As an energy industry professional, he helped me to enter the world of the Non-Governmental Organizations (NGOs), and created the path for me to use my business and technical skills to contribute and bring change to the needy. I truly admired his enthusiasm, can do attitude, and big visions for change. He was about action, not "talk", and this man truly makes things happen!

After studying his approach for a decade, I came to the realization that he had a good model to emulate. I concluded that Subesh really loves Christ, and his Christian beliefs and personal experiences changed him into a caring, servant leader. He got rid of his debts, developed a strong relationship with his God, his wife, and his family. He created a successful and sustainable business, and used this to give back to the world. I want this for myself, and I hope that others through this book, will learn from him .and reach out to others. This is his gift and legacy: genuine love means giving to your neighbours, and in this regard, Subesh and Debbie provide a rich legacy and role model for others to follow. –Winston Mohammed, Santa Margarita Circular, St Augustine

# Post Script

Our dreams, hopes, and anticipations are simple:
Others will reproduce and continue
Sustainable development for
The Anapausis Partnership and
The Bridge of Hope enterprise
And other business ventures,
And develop new efforts as needed;
Based on common sense and faith-based
Principles for the benefit of the children,
Families and the Nation that we both treasure;
As a safe place to grow, develop, and learn
The common-sense lessons necessary for
A productive life.

~

Perhaps more appropriate to the remedial and surrogate caregiver is an answer to these questions:

1. Do individuals have control over the acts that determine their future? Do they need continued guidance and support to make an adequate transition to the real world?

2. Does a caregiver have the potential to undo or over-write the negative programming of a child and thus effect a better and more productive future? If so, can we afford to permit a failed transition and undo the good efforts of so many?

3. What can you do to assist this cause?

# THE ANAPAUSIS SOCIETY ENROLLMENT

### A
Alpha Couples committed to the vision

### B
Beta Males committed to the mission
Beta Females committed to the mission

### Ω
Omega Couples committed to the cause
Omega Males committed to the cause
Omega Females committed to the cause

# PLEDGE OF FIDELITY

I (we) do solemnly affirm before God and these witnesses a firm commitment to the faith-based principles and the teamwork ethic necessary to maintain and strengthen the Anapausis vision for the benefit of Trinidad and Tobago and the Caribbean Region. In addition to placing my signature in the ANAPAUSIS SOCIETY Register, I (we) sign the Pledge of Fidelity and affirm a personal faithfulness and dependability with a solemn vow to keep this promise with the support and strength of a Loving God.

Signature _____ Date

Signature _____ Date

Two Witnesses _____

_____

# HONOREES

THE SOCIETY WILL FROM TIME TO TIME
SELECT AND HONOR INDIVIDUALS AND
ORGANIZATIONS WHICH SHARE THE VISION
AND PARTICIPATE IN THE MISSION
OF CARING FOR THE NEEDY. THE PRIMARY
DATES FOR HONORS AND AWARDS WILL BE
JANUARY 25 AND AUGUST 13.
THE BASIS FOR ALL AWARDS AND HONORS
DEPENDS ON FOUR (4) AREAS OF
DEMONSTRATED STRENGTH: VISION,
COURAGE, INTEGRITY, AND PERSEVERANCE.

THE LOVE GATE

## THE LOVE GATE AWARD

**(To someone who has shown extraordinary love to the children of Trinidad and Tobago.)**

# THE SOCIETY HONOR FOR PARTNERSHIP

**(For those stakeholders and corporate sponsors who partner with projects for the common good.)**

# THE HONEYBEE AWARD

**(Individuals from humble beginnings who began a business and continue to produce to serve the common good.)**

# APPENDICES

Appendix A – Common-sense Lessons

Appendix B – Faith-based Principles

Appendix C – Milestones on the Journey

Appendix D – Residential Children's Homes in Trinidad

Appendix E – Author Resume and Professional History

# Appendix A

## *Common-sense Lessons*

These common-sense lessons were learned from growing up in village life, family relations, work experience, and interpersonal communications in the real world. It is such lessons that prepare young men and women for a life as a productive citizen and parent. All champions of history have learned and used such lessons to make personal advances and to change the world for the better. The common-sense lessons that became faith-based principles that were used to create programs, to construct buildings, and to change the hopes and dreams of disadvantaged children and dysfunctional families could be transferred and reproduced around the world to make a difference in the lives of children, young people and family life.

**Lessons From Early Childhood:**
- ❖ **There is positive value in working together.**
- ❖ **Hard work is a necessary part of life.**
- ❖ **The joint labor of two produces more than the efforts of a solitary worker.**
- ❖ **Companionship and teamwork are both supportive and profitable.**
- ❖ **Value both family and friends.**
- ❖ **Friends are better than money in the bank.**
- ❖ **Foundational instructions must include morality and ethics.**
- ❖ **Serious study even by pitch oil lamps and homemade flambeaux lights are good foundation stones for life.**
- ❖ **Exposure to organized athletics provides foundational rules and regulations of teamwork, cooperation, and the desire to play fair and win.**
- ❖ **There is no end to the benefits of true friendship.**

- ❖ Learning the value of sharing, proper hygiene, eating the same thing that others ate, and wearing hand-me-downs for clothes are good lessons for life.
- ❖ Rising early each morning to see men going to work prepared to provide an honest day's labor is a positive lesson for future employment.
- ❖ Personally working in the family garden provides an appreciation for living and growing things.
- ❖ Learning good housekeeping during the growing years is a lesson with great benefits.
- ❖ Neither race nor religion should divide the people.
- ❖ A good foundation for life is to value family and neighbors.
- ❖ Sharing what one has with others is part of an honest life.
- ❖ Playtime is a great gift to the children when they learn to play without prejudice.
- ❖ Sacrificial gifts of parents teach valuable lessons to the children.
- ❖ A gift is valued by what it costs the giver.
- ❖ Learning that life has a single focus provides a life without distractions.
- ❖ Patience is a virtue children must learn early.
- ❖ Learning the value of music, love, and laughter is necessary for a productive life.
- ❖ Learning the value of work and the worth of money is required for mature living.
- ❖ Learning to earn, save, and spend money is a good foundation for life.
- ❖ Energy spent in a task increases the value of the coin the labor produced.
- ❖ There is no free lunch. One must earn their bread by honest labor.

❖ Learning practical lessons from grandparents are things children can never learn in school.

❖ Many of the hard lessons learned as children become the valued basis for moral and ethical living as an adult

❖ Lessons from the previous generation are always seasoned with experience and mixed with genuine affection.

❖ Grandmothers have a special ability to imprint their character and morality on their grandchildren.

~

## Lessons From Youthful Struggles:

❖ Armed with the practical skills learned from the family, the young can venture into the world of work.

❖ Family members should always encourage the enterprise of the young.

❖ Early discipline and study provides the courage to persevere in the adult world.

❖ Encouragement at home is a strong motivation for the young to venture into the larger world.

❖ Learning to live within the means of the family is essence of morality in life and business.

❖ Learning never to take advantage of others is the first lesson in maturity.

❖ Early work experiences teach the young to bloom where they are planted.

❖ Learning that life has stages that include learning and doing is essential to a productive life.

❖ Learning to accept the assistance of family members is a good lesson.

❖ Each successful task moves one up the ladder of achievement.

❖ The mastering of the skills in one job prepares one for better position.

❖ The lessons learned from extended family and early work will add value to the whole of life and prepare one for the difficulties that come in the adult years.

❖ Facing the reality of death early in life prepares one for the limitations of time and energy.

❖ Life and work have many unexpected lessons that prepare one for the next phase of the journey.

❖ Each common-sense lesson prepares the young for a life of teamwork and cooperation.

❖ Armed with practical childhood lessons, young people are ready to take a forward step into the adult world.

❖ Developing a passion for the beauty of nature brings balance to life.

# Appendix B
## *Faith-based Principles*

These faith-based principles come from sacred writings, friends, and life-experience and have become controlling values for life and living. Readers are challenged to apply these principles to all aspects of their life and work.

---

### Faith-based Principles

**"Two are better than one for they have a good reward for their labor"**
Ω
**"God, show me where your cause needs me most,"**
Ω
**"Write the vision; make it plain"**
Ω
**"Your spouse is a gift from God."**
Ω
**"If you release what is in your hands for God, then He will release what is in His hands for you."**
Ω
**"Take care of God's business and God will take care of your business."**
Ω
**"Look beyond the challenges of broken lives to the potential for a better life."**
Ω
**"No one including the poor and needy cares how much you know until you can convince them of how much you care."**

**"God never wastes a hurt."**
Ω
**"God is a God of 'another chance' not just a second chance."**
Ω
**"God blesses you to be a blessing to others."**

"God calls us to be faithful, not successful."

Ω

"Normally we do not use the word "success" because
it suggests more than enough; one can never do
more than is needed."

Ω

"God's work done God's way never lacks God's supply."

Ω

"Your influence is positive when you are a good example in all
aspects of life."

Ω

"Lead by example in every aspect of both personal and
professional life."

Ω

"Grow and blossom where you are planted."

Ω

"It is not go and do, but do as you go; in reality it is work in your
own environment, in your Jerusalem."

Ω

"Look around you there are needy children in close
proximity to you."

Ω

"It has been said that a human being can live about 40 days
without food, four days without water, and four minutes without
air: but only a miserable life without hope."

Ω

"Every human one meets regardless of their station in life can
add something worthwhile to ones knowledge and experience."

Ω

"Never look at a half full glass; see it filled, half with something
and half with air.  Then come to the knowledge that God is
spirit and fills the whole world and that the balance of a half-
full glass is filled with the spirit and presence of God."

Ω

"Never be inconsistent in dealing with disadvantaged children;
they have already witnessed sufficient discrepancy and
contradiction in their previous environment."

Ω

"Invest in people, property and poverty; the increase in
value is worthy of the effort and has a good
return on the investment."

Ω

"The future of children in Trinidad and Tobago is in our hands."

Ω

"Live a life larger than yourself and work together with God in
the areas of the greatest need."

Ω

"Money cannot purchase happiness, but it can pay the bills."

Ω

"There is a good reward for hard work especially when the
bottom line is to assist the less fortunate."

Ω

"Give to support the ministry of others, but realize that your
personal talents are needed to produce constructive
projects to serve the needy."

Ω

"The state of a nation is not judged by the infrastructure and
buildings but by the prevalent attitude toward infants, children,
families and the less fortunate."

Ω

"Without developing the children into moral and honorable
citizens, there will be no viable state."

Ω

"God put us together not only to help each other, but to work
together for the good of others."

Ω

"Hard work is required to access the funds God provides."

Ω

"Tithing and giving multiplies the nest egg and enables one
to care for the needy."

Ω

"One should tithe both time and talent."

Ω

"Bypass greed and give back to the need."

Ω

"The future of children in Trinidad and Tobago is in our hands."

"A workaholic temperament could be an
advantage to Kingdom building."

Ω

"A Believing wife means a faith-partner."

Ω

"You don't have to make headlines to make a difference."

Ω

"The life you live day by day can make a difference and
impact those around you."

Ω

"Everybody does wrong things; look for the right."

Ω

"You cannot give something you do not have."

Ω

"Try to experience the Lord first each day."

# Appendix C
## *Milestones on the Journey*

**Milestones on the Journey**
*By Subesh Ramjattan, 25th January 2009*

**Paying tribute to the Lord
And dear friends along the journey.**

### Sowing the Seed

1. **25TH January 1998** – "The House of Young Christians" was founded with the original intent of being a "boys' home". After meeting the first family of three boys and three girls, the Lord led us to establish a home for boys and girls.

2. **March 1998** – The 3-acre property on Mohammed Street was purchased, and the Lord guided us in building The Anapausis Community.

3. **13th August 1999** – Dedication of the "Fellowship Hall" in honour of my wife, Debbie, who supported me in the vision God gave us for Anapausis.

### Tending the Vision

1. **25th January 2001** – In response to God's call, ordination as ministers of the Gospel by Drs. Robert & Glenyce Doorn through Kingsway Fellowship International.

2. **25th January 2001** – Dedication of the Anapausis Chapel in honour of Papa & Mama Doorn.

3. **25th January 2002** – Dedication of the FamilyLife & Support Center for the purpose of family restoration and education. This is part of the Anapausis vision.

4. **17ᵗʰ April 2003** – The Lord opened the way for us to purchase 5 acres of land on Eastern Main Road, James Smart Village and we started construction of "Bridge of Hope" (formerly "House of Young Christians").

5. **October 2003** – Dedication of a classroom in honor of the precious legacy received from my parents Rosie and Dipnarine Ramjattan.

**Soaring in His purpose!**

1. **25ᵗʰ January 2004** – Dedication of "Bridge of Hope" Children's Home & Community Services.

2. **25ᵗʰ January 2007** – Dedication of a storage room at the "House of Marketing Limited", Arima, to receive and distribute goods to the less fortunate, connecting those in need with God's loving provision.

3. **25ᵗʰ January 2007** – Commissioning of Johnson & Johnson Community Medical Room at Bridge of Hope

4. **June 2008** – The privilege of serving on a project in the UK and assisting as trustee in setting up "LifeLine Foundation UK", a registered charity.

5. **24ᵗʰ January 2009** – Prayer dedication of "Kernahan Village Resource Center."

6. **25ᵗʰ January 2010** – Dedication of Education and Developmental Assessment Centre

7. **12ᵗʰ April 2010** – Launch of the Anapausis Society to preserve the legacy.

8. **25ᵀᴴ January 2011** – THE ANAPAUSIS PARTNERSHIP book published in honor of Subesh's Birthday.

# Appendix D
## *Childrens' Homes in Trinidad and Tobago*

### NORTH
NAME, Town/District

**ST. MICHAEL'S SCHOOL FOR BOYS,**
Diego Martin

**ST. JUDE'S SCHOOL FOR GIRLS,** Belmont

**ST. DOMINIC'S CHILDREN'S HOME,** Belmont

**HOLY NAME GIRLS' TRAINING CENTRE,**
Port of Spain

**MARIAN HOUSE,** Port of Spain

**CREDO DROP-IN & DEVELOP'TAL CENTRE,**
Port of Spain

**SOPHIA HOUSE,** Port of Spain

**AYLWARD HOUSE,** Gonzales

**OUR LADY OF THE WAYSIDE,** Belmont

**RAINBOW RESCUE,** Port of Spain

**EMMANUEL CRADLE,** Woodbrook

**CHRIST CHILD CONVALESCENT HOME,**
Diego Martin

### EAST

**ARK OF THE COVENANT,** Success Village,
Laventille

**ST. DOMINIC'S "SUNNY HILL HOMESTEAD",**
Barataria

**ST. DOMINIC'S "PLAIN VIEW HOMESTEAD"**,
Arima

**AMICA**, St. Augustine

**ST. MARY'S CHILDREN'S HOME**, Tacariqua

**RAFFA HOUSE FOR BOYS**, Curepe

**RAFFA HOUSE FOR GIRLS**, Tacariqua

**HOUSE OF GRACE**, Arima

**JESUS CARES FAMILY COTTAGE**,
Malabar, Arima

**MARGARET KISTOW CHILDREN'S HOME**,
Malabar, Arima

**JOSHUA BOYS'**, Santa Rosa Heights, Arima

**HEART OF MARY CARE CENTRE**,
Sangre Grande

**CASA DE CORAZON (HEART HOME)**,
Sangre Grande

**BRIDGE OF HOPE**, James Smart Village,
Sangre Chiquito

# CENTRAL

**SRI JAYALAKSHMI CHILDREN'S HOME**,
Longdenville

**ANGELS ON EARTH FOUNDATION**,
Chaguanas

**ANGEL MICHAEL HOSTEL FOR YOUTHS**,
Chaguanas

**COUVA CHILDREN'S HOME & CRISIS NURSERY**,
Couva

**EZEKIEL CHILDREN'S HOME**, Preysal Village, Couva

**GRACE CHILDREN'S HOME**,
Beaucarro Village, Freeport

**DAR UL AMAN FREEPORT CHILDREN'S HOME**, Freeport

**WESLEYAN CHILDREN'S HOME, FLORENCE FOUNDATION**, Upper Carapichaima

## TOBAGO

**SYLPHIL HOME IN LOVE**, Scarborough

## SOUTH

**ISLAMIC HOME FOR CHILDREN**, Bonneventure

**OPERATION SMILE**, Williamsville

**EL SHADDAI RESTORATION HOME**,
Bonne Adventure

**HOPE CENTRE**, Point a Pierre

**MOTHERS' UNION CHILDREN'S HOME**,
San Fernando

**ST. MARIA GORRETTI CHILDREN'S HOME**,
St. Mary's Village, Oropuche

**OUTSTRETCH HANDS CENTER OF LIFE**,
Borde Narve, Princes Town

**SWAHA CHILDREN'S HOME**, Penal

**HAPPY HOME FOR CHILDREN**, Majuba Hill,
La Brea

**FERNDEAN CHILDREN'S HOME**, Harriman Park,
Pt Fortin

# SPECIALLY CHALLENGED

## PHYSICALLY CHALLENGED

PRINCESS ELIZABETH CENTRE, Woodbrook

## MENTALLY CHALLENGED

LADY HOCHOY HOME, Cocorite

## BLIND / VISUALLY IMPAIRED

SCHOOL FOR BLIND CHILDREN, Santa Cruz

## DEAF / HEARING IMPAIRED

CASCADE SCHOOL FOR THE DEAF, Cascade

## HIV / AIDS

CYRIL ROSS HOME FOR CHILDREN, Tunapuna

## PREGNANT TEENS

MARY CARE CENTRE, Woodbrook

## CHILDREN & YOUTH AT RISK

FAMILY FIRST FOUNDATION, Scarborough, Tobago

## HANDICAPPED / MULTIPLE

MISSIONARIES OF CHARITY, Success Village, Laventille

BLESSED QUIETNESS HOME, Glencoe

## CONDUCT DISORDER CENTRE

PETHERTON TRUST, New Grant, Princess Town

Notes :

Data was originally prepared by Carol Almarales,  Tel: (868)- 667-0912, or E-mail: ckalmarales@tstt.net.tt
Extracted by Edison Hoolasie for  Subesh Ramjattan, Tel: 868-678-7748, or E-mail: ehoolasie@tstt.net.tt

# Appendix E
## *Resumé and Professional History*

### SUBESH RAMJATTAN

#1 ANAPAUSIS - MOHAMMED STREET, CUREPE -
TRINIDAD & TOBAGO

HOME: 868-663-3518    MOBILE: 868-354-7319
E-MAIL: SUBESH60@GMAIL.COM

## VISION

- Continue to contribute to local and regional development, by empowering those at risk, developing life skills for the youth, promoting strong ethics and governance, and building and sustaining strong marriages and families.

- Mentor and build future leaders in philanthropy and community development

- Promote a broad-based policy for the development of children from childhood to professional and higher education achievements in Trinidad and Tobago.

- Develop a general program of juvenile socialization with committed service providers and volunteers who supply the care, nurture, education, and skills training needed to gain the age-specific development necessary to function adequately and make Trinidad and Tobago a safe society for children to live and grow.

## PERSONAL PROFILE

- A pioneer in building communities through social support structures at the Bridge of Hope, Children's Villages Association of Trinidad and Tobago, and the Kernahan Centre for Community Development.

- An advocate for building and sustaining strong family life through personal leadership and investments in FamilyLife of Trinidad and Tobago.

- A successful entrepreneur with a proven track record for building and operating businesses based on sound ethics, governance practices, and social responsibility.

## PHILANTROPHY

**1998 – Present: Founder/ Chief Executive Officer , The Bridge of Hope**

*Objective: Improving the lives of at risk children and empowering communities on the Eastern Seaboard of Trinidad and Tobago*

- Bridge of Hope site developed in James Smart Village at a cost of $5,500,000 with facilities for a 32-bed children's home, Community Resource Centre, and a Micro Enterprise Development centre.

- Over the last 10 years, provided a home and caring environment for at least 150 abandoned and abused children.

- Based on several needs analyses, enabled various community services and programmes:

  - Pre-school in collaboration with Servol and Petroleum Women's Club

  - Image Skills Centre for developing Aesthetic skills in young women from the Home and surrounding communities, in partnership with the IADB, Sacha Cosmetics and the Australian High Commission

  - Computer Literacy classes in conjunction with NESC for the children and local communities in the eastern seaboard

- Community Health Room in collaboration with Johnson & Johnson and medical volunteers to provide free health care to the children and communities

- Agriculture projects to sustain food production for the Bridge of Hope Children's Home and to build agricultural life skills in the children.

**2009 – Present:  Director / Founder,
Kernahan Centre for Community Development**

*Objective: Creating a framework to improve the quality of life of people in Kernahan, Cascadoux and other communities along the South East Coast*

- Kernahan Centre for Community Development (KCCD) established legally as an NGO, with fully functional board of directors and governance systems, and provided a framework for corporate sponsors, NGOs, government agencies, private individuals to support the needs of these communities

  - 1st Phase of the Project oversaw the construction of a pre-school and a Community Resource Centre at a cost of $1,500,000.00 partially funded by BPTT on 10,000 sq ft of land donated by the Cocal Estate

  - A Pre School, in collaboration with Servol, now provides the opportunity for 20 children to access education for the first time

  - A homework and computer center to provide coaching and educational support for children and their parents to improve their literacy and chances of success at school.

  - Parent outreach programme in partnership with Servol.

**1998 – Present: Director / Founder,
The Anapausis Community**

*Objective: Creating a legacy and model of philanthropy
and partnership*

- Anapausis Community site established on 3 acres of
  land in St Augustine, with buildings and facilities that
  hosts community activities and support several non-
  governmental organizations:

  - FamilyLife and Support Centre that facilitates
    marriage counselling and support through
    Home Builders cell groups and annual Marriage
    Conferences

  - OASIS Institute of Higher Learning, accredited with
    the Ministry of Education (Accrediting Council of
    Trinidad and Tobago) to provide graduate degree
    programmes in FamilyLife Education, Organizational
    Leadership, and Educational Measurement.

  - ICAN - International Children's Academy for Neo-
    development to enhance children's cognitive and
    learning development

  - Caribbean Psycho-educational Assessment
    Services Ltd to perform psycho-educational
    evaluations and assessment services

  - Campus Crusade for Christ local and regional
    offices for supporting students at tertiary
    institutions

  - Through the Anapausis Community, funds have
    been invested in improving marriages, improving
    children's health and well being, and in building
    capacity in these NGOs

  - Over 4,000 persons have directly and indirectly
    been assisted through programs and services from
    this site and its activities in the last 5 years

**2002- Present: Chairman of the Board of Governors, Oasis University**

A Trinidad and Tobago based graduate program offering master's and doctorates to individuals serving in the social professions.

## BUSINESS EXPERIENCE

**1976 - Present:  Managing Director / Founder, The House of Marketing Ltd.**

- Built from ground up, a sustainable and successful business that supplies and installs acoustical and flooring products.  Our motto: "Under promise and over deliver."

*Established other divisions:*
- The House of Marketing Interiors
- The House of Marketing Engineering
- The House of Marketing Partitions
- The House of Marketing (San Fernando) Ltd.
- The House of Marketing Electronics
- The House of Marketing Lumber and Plywood
- Drapery Land
- Floor Covering Distributors Inc., Miami, Florida, USA (1980 – 1993)
- MINI Enterprises Inc., Miami, Florida Fla., USA (1980-1993)

**1980-1993: Founder. North American Carpet Mills, Chatsworth, Georgia, USA**

- Distribution network in the Caribbean and in the Tri-County of Florida (Dade, Broward & Palm Beach)

**Other Employment History**

- Bata Shoe Company Ltd./Trinidad Footwear Company Ltd. 1968 – 1971
- Stock keeper, Customs Clerk, Purchasing and Costing Clerk, and Production Supervisor
- Accounts Clerk, Singer Sewing Machine Company Limited 1972 – 1973
- Purchasing Manager, Sampton Metal Limited (Subsidiary of Neal and Massy Company Ltd.) 1973 – 1975
- Route Sales Manager for Coca Cola Limited (Subsidiary of Cannings Foods Limited) 1975 –Sept. 1976

## PROFESSIONAL DEVELOPMENT

- Ordained Minister – Kingsway Fellowship International Des Moines, Iowa, USA, 14th January 1999
- Successfully graduated from the Management Development Centre – July 1983

    - Marketing Research & Planning
    - Product Planning & Pricing
    - Distribution
    - Marketing Organisation & Control
    - Marketing Communication
    - Export Marketing
    - Market Forecasting
    - The Marketing Budget & Budgetary Control
    - Environmental issues as they affect present Day Marketing
    - Organisation  Operation of A Marketing Department

- Junior Executive Course – Bata Shoe Co. Ltd., October 1970
- G.C.E. O'Levels: Spanish, Mathematics, Principles of Accounts, English Literature, English Language, History
- 1962–1967 North Eastern College Sangre Grande, Trinidad and Tobago

## Awards and Honours

Sangre Grande Regional Corporation – Independence Day Community Work 2000

March 2003 Baccalaureate of Studies (BSt) OASIS UNIVERSITY

Recipient of the True Heroes Association, Love and Dedication Shown Toward Children – May 2003

July 2010 Doctor of Humane Letters (DHL) OASIS Institute of Higher Learning

## Interests:

Table Tennis, Cricket, Football, Swimming, Billiards, All Fours.

## PERSONAL INFORMATION

**Date of Birth:** January 25th, 1951

**Marriage Status:** Married to Debra Frost Ramjattan, two children, two grandchildren

# THE ANAPAUSIS PARTNERSHIP
## COMMON-SENSE LESSONS AND FAITH-BASED PRINCIPLES
## THAT RESULT IN A MODEL OF
## PHILANTHROPY, MENTORING, AND COACHING

**Subesh and Debra Ramjattan**

**ISBN 978-1-935434-49-8**

GREEN WINE
FAMILY BOOKS

**A Division of**
**GlobalEdAdvancePRESS**